D0903180

Rob -

Amazing to mee -

you - looking

forward to more

time together!

-Sa

Solving the Giving Pledge Bottleneck

Sean Davis

Solving the Giving Pledge Bottleneck

How to Finance Social and
Environmental Challenges Using
Venture Philanthropy at Scale

palgrave
macmillan

Sean Davis
Merton Capital Partners
Jupiter, FL, USA

ISBN 978-3-030-78864-3   ISBN 978-3-030-78865-0   (eBook)
https://doi.org/10.1007/978-3-030-78865-0

Cover design by Artist 1782/shutterstock

This Palgrave Macmillan imprint is published by the registered company Springer Nature Switzerland AG
The registered company address is: Gewerbestrasse 11, 6330 Cham, Switzerland

To Allegra and Siena, my sunrise and my sunset, and to Alexandra and Sebastian, my tomorrow and my yesterday.

Acknowledgements

I'm grateful to all the Merton advisors for your support and guidance: Robert Boyd, Barnaby Marsh, Guy Cave, Philip DiComo, Paul Schervish, Richard Cosnotti, Kirby Rosplock, Gabriel Rabinovici and Barbara Quasius. Thank you also to William Vernon, Gideon Pfeffer, Robert Aycock, Charles Harris, Alexander Loucopoulos, Upmanu Lall, Henry Jamison IV, Pierre Smith, Paul Coombs, Sandra Barghini, Armando Fana and Paola Roman for your partnership in developing solutions in funding water infrastructure and affordable housing. These have resulted in the largest actionable social justice and equity opportunities available. I also want to thank Patricia Frigo, Stephen Hampe, Damian Walker, Nicolas Guzman, Michael Atwater, Neely Young, Arick Wierson, Beau Standish and Tula Weis at Palgrave Macmillan, for your encouragement and advice.

Thank you also to Geraldine Tafur and Alison Davis for making this possible and thank you to James Finley for all the spiritual bridges you design, especially the one to Thomas Merton. Finally, a thank you to Thomas Merton for continuing to inspire us. You are more relevant today than ever before.

Photographs

David Scarola is a fine art and portrait photographer based in Jupiter, Florida. He travels the world taking pictures of and for clients and adding to his various portfolios. David's inspiration for this work comes from his love of interacting with people, observing wildlife, experiencing different cultures, and exploring exotic and intriguing locations. David is an advocate for the homeless and has worked increase awareness of their suffering through this photography. He is also a passionate environmentalist.

Contents

About the Author

Sean Davis started his career with J. P. Morgan in New York and then joined Advent International, a leader in international private equity, helping to develop its office in Brazil. Mr. Davis then joined Saratoga Partners in New York and was dedicated to leverage buyout opportunities and restructurings. Mr. Davis was recently the Development Director for The Salvation Army of Palm Beach County, where he was focused on creating a bold growth plan to solve the problem that almost half the children in the county fail to read a third grade level. He is the former Director of Major Gifts and Planned Giving for The Lord's Place, a leading organization in the homelessness arena in Palm Beach County. He was also responsible for managing the execution of the housing strategy at The Salvation Army in Palm Beach County and The Lord's Place.

Mr. Davis is the Founder and CEO of Merton Capital Partners. Merton is a leader in creating large-scale vehicles for philanthropic investments. Merton advises philanthropists in deploying their funds to solve our most important social and environmental challenges. Mr. Davis has developed new approaches to help philanthropists including co-investing large philanthropy with leading for-profits in affordable housing, clean water and renewable energy.

Mr. Davis was raised in Colombia and Argentina and graduated from Phillips Exeter Academy and from The Edmund A. Walsh School of Foreign Service at Georgetown University. He also has an MBA from the London Business School where as a student he co-founded the LBS Private Equity Conference and The LBS Coller Institute of Private Equity.

Mr. Davis is a member of the Board of Advisors of NAMI PBC, an affiliate for the National Alliance for Mental Illness and was previously a member of the Board of Directors. In addition, he is an advisor to the Adorer Missionary Sisters of the Poor in Tanzania and an Adjunct Professor in Palm Beach Atlantic University's Masters in Global Development. He lives in Jupiter, Florida, with his family and red retriever.

"Is there to be found on earth a fullness of joy, or is there no such thing? Is there some way to make life fully worth living, or is this impossible? If there is such a way, how do you go about finding it?"
—Thomas Merton

1

Introduction

There has never been an opportunity to finance more good. We are moving into an inflection point where for the first time in history we can finance the specific solutions to the social and environmental challenges dearest to each of us. Tonight in every city and many communities in the U.S., hundreds of mothers are sleeping in their cars with their children in a Walmart parking lot. According to the National Alliance to End Homelessness, there were 12,562 moms with children unsheltered on any given night in 2019 across the country.[1]

If we use estimates based on population, in Florida's Miami-Dade County alone we will find around 200 mothers with their children tonight sleeping in their cars, and many more in shelters. In Palm Beach County, about 100 mothers will do the same, as there are no more available beds, or any funds to provide them with emergency housing, like a motel room, have likely run out. They will be anxiously driving to find a safe place to park, while worrying about gas money and hoping for a clean bathroom that is safe. The fortunate mothers are the ones who will be temporarily sheltered with friends and family. Their goodwill still runs out, just as local funds for motels run out. This is America in 2021.

These numbers may be greatly underestimated as funds to count them, collect, study and report the data are limited and based in large part on the goodwill of volunteers. Many of these volunteers are nonprofit workers who are already working weekends and often needing a second job to continue to battle homelessness. This is one of many unyielding, unrelenting and worsening challenges overwhelming nonprofits as they only have a sliver of the funds needed individually or as a whole to solve their challenges. Tax funding is also only covering another sliver of the need despite there being proven solutions that just need more funding, and many of these save our communities' costs overall and make them much safer and stronger. COVID-19 has made those vulnerable even more so.

This is one of many social and environmental challenges today in every community and globally. This inflection point will change everything. The work we need to focus on now is how do we attract, channel, and effectively deploy the enormous funds emerging looking to do more good. The most visible is The Giving Pledge. The dollars publicly pledged by over 200 of the wealthiest people in the world are estimated at $600 billion,[2] yet they are not flowing into solutions as the giving rates of these individuals are very low. At the same time, their wealth continues to grow creating a tremendous bottleneck. As an example of the high end of this spectrum, Elon Musk's rapid wealth increases in 2021 may put the pledges well over $600 billion.

Corporations, private equity funds and others will also be looking to finance large solutions rather than sponsor incremental good. Incremental good is important; however, financing large-scale solutions is now possible and some of the largest solutions will require partnerships with these corporations and private investors who can deploy larger philanthropic capital for good. Many business and finance leaders are measuring which United Nations SDG goals their company is furthering. That is just a first step. Seeing how they can play a role in partnering with philanthropists in solving those challenges is the new path forward.

According to the Internal Revenue Services, the nonprofit sector accounts for 5.6% of U.S. GDP, and individuals, foundations and corporations gave $427.7 billion in 2018.[3] Nevertheless, most of the philanthropy given in the U.S. is diffused among 1.5 million nonprofits.[4] Even the larger foundations rarely give more than $500,000 to a specific nonprofit in any given year. In 2019, The Ford Foundation had $14.3 billion in funds and gave $463 million in grants. These grants supported the critical work of 2,066 nonprofits and most were less than $250,000 each. 48 grants were larger than $3 million.[5] Scale in giving is a must to solve our challenges. We are beginning to witness scale in giving.

The MacArthur Foundation initiated a grant competition in 2018 which awarded the first $100 million foundation grant to one nonprofit.[6] They are now selecting their second and plan to have a recipient every 2 years in addition to launching Lever for Change, a subsidiary to secure larger funds for more leading nonprofits. Other nonprofits are looking at similar "Big Bets" to scale quicker. However, this is hard to do as there are not that many nonprofits that can readily take in and quickly expand their operations with $100 or $200 million.

The individuals who have signed The Giving Pledge, led by Bill and Melinda Gates and Warren Buffet, have taken a leap of faith in order to inspire others to also do more. This is one part of the rising tide of good in these seemingly distressing times. Yet it is a time of great hope, as our societies are changing and this rising tide is beginning to accelerate. We must focus on developing effective solutions to our challenges. These are actual, quantifiable and visible large-scale solutions.

After working in and around the challenges of homelessness, urban poverty, early learning, affordable housing and mental health for the last 10 years, I have seen what is simply a chronic underfunding of solutions. Many successful solutions already exist and simply need scale. However, scale can be elusive but not impossible to achieve. There is a clear underinvesting in affordable housing, homeless services, education and job training that are easy to see. According to the Annie E. Casey Foundation, 68% of 4th grade children in the U.S. could not read at grade level.[7] This is astonishing.

More fundamentally, there is a chronic underinvestment, and sometimes, a complete lack of investment in planning. Ask your local homeless nonprofit for the specific dollar amount they need to house these mothers and their children in your community for one night. How about permanently? Or the veterans. Ask the leading early child nonprofit leaders for the dollar amount need to have all the children in your community reading at 3rd or 4th grade level every fall. The latter is a question of more teachers, buses and buildings that can be managed through a nonprofit. The kind of growth needed requires management teams with experience in managing exponential growth and it begins with developing a detailed long-term growth plan. If there were an individual willing to write the very large check to fund this solution, most nonprofits would not have the detailed growth plan needed to scale. The amount to catch up all the children in Palm Beach County, is $176 million.

These management teams would love to fulfill their organizational missions and yet they have never had the luxury to create a detailed plan, as they scramble to keep the lights on or meet this year's budget. There is thus very little in what for-profit financial experts would consider detailed planning in the nonprofit world. This has now changed. The Giving Pledge funds could be used to create detailed large growth plans and deliver high-impact solutions.

The mothers who are homeless in your community are often victims of domestic violence, and many were evicted following the loss of a job or large hospital bill that sent their finances into a tailspin. They were likely already forced to choose between food, buying medicine, or spending a restful and safe night in a motel. Tonight they may be considering worse and horrific options. What would they do in order to take their children to a motel tonight? I have had to tell mothers with children that our family shelters and all those across the county were full.

Seeing them drive away without hope in a car with all their possessions is a tragedy that will repeat itself at least 12,000 times today in the U.S. It was a good day when there were funds to pay for one or two nights in a motel room. Mostly, they were not good days. On the same day that I would have to see those mothers drive away, I would visit donors in Palm Beach looking to raise funds to provide these mothers with a temporary solution. But where were the permanent solutions?

An additional 52,000 families are sheltered in homeless shelters across America.[7] Some will receive temporary housing and support, and that is all that a few of them need. But over 60% of them will exit these short-term stays with no prospect of permanent housing beyond their friends, family, cars, the street or other overcrowded shelters.[8] Within these dire challenges, there are even more tragic challenges in terms of gender, sexual orientation and race. Solutions are also more complex when these challenges intersect with severe mental health issues, incarceration and human trafficking. However, solutions can be found today.

Beyond the mothers already on the streets, there is a tragic number of potential homeless mothers hanging on to their homes in a sea of poverty in the U.S. today. In May of 2019, the Federal Reserve released their report on the Economic Well-Being of U.S. Households. This report included a well-publicized finding that almost 40% of Americans do not have the ability to pay for an unexpected expense of $400.[9] Most of our healthcare and social support systems are overrun with demands for food, shelter, financial support, health services and more. Tonight there are girls and boys with unimaginable trauma who are turning 18 and aging out of foster care, and becoming homeless on their birthdays. They are no longer able to stay with their foster families and the shelters are likely full.

Beyond the social challenges that have solutions already, there is an another set of environmental challenges with solutions. Tonight, there are over 21 million Americans with polluted water in their faucets.[9] Also, 46% of U.S. rivers are polluted.[10] Despite the growing and seemingly endless environmental degradation, there is a constant and persistent desire to reverse the damage to our ecosystems. And here solutions already exist too. Many of these solutions can be both self-sustaining and delivered at enormous scale.

The philanthropy to finance large solutions has always been limited and hard to find. Nonprofits, large and small, have had to take on these challenges with shoestring budgets and limited teams. The front-line social workers do not have the funds and cannot scale solutions to provide help once their residential facilities are at capacity and funds for a motel and for rent assistance run out. Yet they are still there providing kindness and emotional support.

Today is a new day in global philanthropy. We are moving towards a time when more individuals give much of their fortunes to provide the funds to scale solutions. Funding solutions is becoming a new way of measuring their success beyond being the wealthiest entrepreneurs and business leaders. Their funds will also be catalysts to unlock larger corporate philanthropy and to encourage more targeted government grants as the cost savings of these solutions are proven further. This philanthropy still needs to be attracted and cultivated, and this can be extremely challenging.

Innovation does not always proceed in a straight line, and today is the time for innovation in financial scale for good to not just alleviate, but solve many of the world's challenges. Philanthropists looking to give billions of philanthropy are having a difficult time giving it away. A few like Charles Feeney, MacKenzie Scott and Bill and Melinda Gates have found their way; yet, these are just a few who have pledged to give billions. Nobody wants their fortune to be used in a way that does not have great impact. For the longest time, it has been very time consuming and complex to generate large impact, especially if someone wants to fund a ground-breaking solution.

All philanthropy is important. All nonprofit work is important. Matching those philanthropists who want to fund solutions is critical to actually solving these challenges. As we work towards solutions, more specialized talent is needed in growing organizations, structuring deals, partnering with Fortune 500 companies, private equity firms, large for-profit affordable housing developers to have them deploy these large funds quickly and efficiently. This can also reduce the risk of executing on these solutions as they are already sustainable, as they are for-profit companies. It is therefore better to scale the solutions by blending philanthropy in projects led by for-profits nationally and globally.

In this book, I'll be using the term nonprofits for any 501(c)(3) organizations, which are also referred to as mission-driven organizations or a series of other terms. Some of the latter can be confused with for-profit companies which have an impact component or were primarily created to pursue impact such as B Corps (certified B corporations).

Because of decades of society discouraging nonprofits from investing in their management and systems, large philanthropists are generally not regularly being offered opportunities to solve these challenges with detailed 10-year growth plans showing how $200 million in philanthropy can solve the challenge nonprofits were created to tackle. The great news is that this is now starting to change. As I write this, MacKenzie Scott is showing the world how over $8 billion can be given in a span of a few months to hundreds of organizations with few strings attached and trusting their management teams to use it wisely.

Like MacKenzie Scott, some cutting-edge mega-philanthropists are looking to make much larger and more targeted gifts to scale organizations and move towards measurable solutions. They are teaming up with other mega-philanthropists to increase their giving and to fund specialized organizations to deploy the funds according to detailed long-term plans, high accountability and high levels of value-added assistance beyond funds. These philanthropists understand that nonprofit management teams need help creating detailed long-term plans and help to prepare for growth at rates not ever possible before.

Big Bets also need to develop sustainable "exits" once a $200 million ten-year scale up of a leading nonprofit has been completed. The nonprofit needs to replace these funds with forms of sustainable revenue. These include encouraging governments to fund the solutions once they are proven. This greater spending can be better justified to taxpayers as the cost savings or tangible benefits to the community can be seen and structured as performance contracts. We are past the 10-year point of the first Social Impact Bond launched in the U.K. to create funding mechanisms for governments to finance nonprofit interventions with private capital. As the cost savings to the government were realized, they would pay back the investors with a return. Other innovative approaches include The Nature Conservancy's "Blue Bonds," successfully having island countries like the Seychelles permanently set aside thousands of miles of coastline in exchange for them helping to restructure their national debt.[11]

How do you prepare a nonprofit to double in size if it has only grown at modest rates for decades? Can they manage sustained increases in scale? Who has experience in their teams to upgrade all their systems which can cripple the highest performing publicly-traded company if poorly executed? Greatly scaling nonprofits is a specialized art and a science, similar to private equity investments in the restructuring world. Early in my career I worked for Advent International and Saratoga Partners, both private equity firms where we made restructuring investments in Brazil and the U.S. We were looking at acquiring companies that needed to make significant financial or operational changes or sometimes both. This added a very serious level of complexity above traditional private equity investments in companies that were doing well and thriving.

Fortunately, there is already a small crop of organizations that are acting as value-added private equity firms with philanthropy. They are bringing together large philanthropists to give together and to give recipients of the funds help beyond just funds. This model of direct investing, like private equity, is much more complex and time consuming than issuing grants in the traditional philanthropic model. It requires specialized teams to do the time-consuming work of helping nonprofit teams develop long-term plans showing in detail what $200 million deployed into their nonprofit looks like over 10 years. These outsourced advisors also have to do the hard work of collecting the funds from the various philanthropists.

Committing to fund a 10-year plan to scale a nonprofit is just the beginning of a long process in "Big Bets." Third-party organizations, convening philanthropists and supporting nonprofit management teams, have already been in existence at the "venture" level giving mostly grants of less than $1 million. Venture philanthropy organizations have been playing this role for 20 years. Venture philanthropy lost its shine in the last few years as larger impact was not seen as clearly as the success of their cousin firms in the venture capital space who funded companies that became Amazon, Airbnb and Google. Venture philanthropy was also believed to solve all challenges and it is not the case, especially at the venture level. Nor is it at larger levels.

Without the prospect of massive profits, smaller nonprofits cannot grow as much. The difference is that unlike share values going up as the prospects of high profits explode for some venture capital investments into the next eBay, nonprofits almost always need more philanthropy in order to grow. The larger the scale, the more nonprofits need funding. There are exceptions to these in nonprofits which can generate significant funds in their operation, such as some in education and others like hospitals; but even they need more philanthropy to grow and compete with private peers.

The field of venture philanthropy has seen successful applications of the private equity investment process to nonprofits at relatively smaller gift sizes. The Giving Pledge, with its ground-breaking inspirational impact, has opened the doors of mega-philanthropy to be available for such direct philanthropic investments. A new later stage field of venture philanthropy firms is arising focused on much larger gifts. This is an important step in the institutionalization of philanthropic investing. There are many more pieces that need to be developed to accelerate the deployment of funds and help philanthropists large and small have more opportunities presented to them in an efficient manner.

If we want more solutions, nonprofits need more specialized talent, and we need to attract that talent from the for-profit world at competitive rates. No talent, no growth. Thankfully, with the advent of The Giving Pledge, the shift towards solving problems shows how aligned incentives are the fastest path to reducing human suffering and solving climate change. As the philanthropic world grows and becomes more institutionalized, the volumes of funds allow for all the organizations, companies and firms to attract talent remunerated on a for-profit standard. All benefit, and most of all, those suffering today and the planet. The most successful entrepreneurs, business and finance leaders that created their fortunes aligning incentives and backing top talent understand this. The shift from shoestring budgets to skilled talent in growing organizations, to get solutions done, is possible simply by philanthropists willing it. It is the win–win path and the path for them to generate the most fulfilment in seeing solutions happen that are at scale, impactful and visible.

Philanthropy is the largest unmanaged pool of capital in terms of direct investing. Foundations give grants mostly without requiring the time-intensive work at the nonprofit that large growth requires. Venture philanthropists take months in helping nonprofit teams develop long-term detailed growth plans, and supporting them to implement them over the long-term. This very active approach is akin to the private equity process except the funds are not generating a financial return. They are generating fulfilment, a fullness of joy in the donor as social and environmental impact is attained. Yet the funds do need to be invested into a company (the nonprofit) and the management teams need support to go to the next level.

Larger venture philanthropy also benefits from philanthropists looking to solve entire challenges. The traditional mindset of giving and expecting nonprofits to operate on a shoestring budget is changing. These large growth plans build-in all the resources needed to scale. These innovating philanthropists understand that the operational challenges require both sophisticated and experienced management teams and venture philanthropists. There is a need for unrestricted mega-gifts, helping nonprofits do more of what they already do well. There is also a need for larger targeted mega-gifts provided with active management support to attain actual solutions.

Although some noteworthy philanthropists are looking to meet their Giving Pledge commitments on their own, most may want to outsource this intensive work to large venture philanthropists who are experienced in deploying funds at scale in projects of $100 million and above. Similarly to investing in the funds of Sequoia or Kleiner, Perkins to benefit from finding the next Amazon or Apple, deploying enough philanthropy through large venture philanthropy firms may solve some of our social and environmental challenges locally and globally.

Philanthropy is no different. If we are to actually deploy all the funds committed today to The Giving Pledge, and funds already committed to Donor Advised Funds, we need to encourage the large venture philanthropy industry to be understood, utilized and grow by attracting those with private equity backgrounds into the field and sharing their experience. More philanthropists are learning that there are professional managers that they can outsource their mega-philanthropy to reduce their risk of not attaining great impact and to maximize fulfilment. If we want more good to be financed, we need more large-scale venture philanthropy. Large venture philanthropy is where the private equity business was in 1950.

At the time, there were no private equity funds and few understood what the active management of funds entailed. Direct investing was not common despite now being in every part of our economy. The Giving Pledge is expected to reach $600 billion in pledged gifts by 2022. This number may be closer to $1 trillion in unmanaged philanthropy today sitting on the sidelines, especially given the large wealth increase of some signers in 2020 and 2021. Tragically, the challenges causing great suffering are also sitting there. The great news is that many have solutions waiting for financial scale.

My goal is to show that both the funds and the solutions to many of our largest social and environmental challenges are already present. We need to engage large philanthropists to let them know this and encourage them to fully engage in the deployment of more of their funds with large venture philanthropists. This will greatly increase their fulfilment as these larger solutions can be seen and the suffering can be visibly ended. Venture philanthropists can deploy gifts at scale both into nonprofits and into for-profit situations where they create great impact. The latter will prove to be the way to deploy the most philanthropy with the most impact. This is the advent of Program Related Investments (PRI) at scale.

The blending of philanthropy into for-profits (PRI) has been taking place for decades. Blended finance has also been greatly done at the venture level by USAID, The Bill & Melinda Gates Foundation and many others. My work is mostly focused now on blending philanthropy into for-profit situations where we can benefit from these companies' abilities to take in large funds and deliver tremendous measurable impact.

Their management teams have long track records of growth and they are profitable and thus already sustainable, avoiding the "exit" risk in Big Bets. PRIs are allowed by the IRS as a good is taking place and these types of investments allow philanthropy to be invested in larger amounts and at faster rates. Philanthropists can leverage for-profit companies and management teams to roll out good in very high volumes.

Philanthropy can generate more affordable housing in a sustainable way through PRI with developers. We can deliver housing to specific populations like these mothers and their children in cars tonight. We can leverage both for-profit and nonprofit developers to get there, as they are each motivated to build more. The challenge today is knowing about PRI and committing the funds. We can quantify the exact number of buildings needed nationally or per city to eradicate a social issue while developers deliver the sustainable and beautiful buildings.

With permanent housing retention rates of 80–96%, this legitimately solves homelessness while alleviating the affordable housing challenge to prevent more homelessness. It would take less than 5% of The Giving Pledge funds, co-invested into for-profit affordable housing projects, to deliver all the housing needed nationally to house the homeless. More philanthropic investments are needed to solve homelessness, but we can solve the lack of homeless housing issue, which is the most expensive and capital-intensive part of the solution.

We can also blend philanthropy into acquisitions with PRI at scale. Private water investors purchasing and upgrading water utilities in the U.S. cannot focus on the areas of largest social justice and equity challenges. PRI allow them to purchase and upgrade the 5,000 or so water utilities which are so abandoned they deliver contaminated water to 21 million Americans every day. These private investors cannot buy them without philanthropy as the cost to upgrade their infrastructure is too high, making them uneconomical. They have thousands of other utilities to purchase where they can make their minimum returns.

These 5,000 are in distressed areas with also the highest environmental inequality and struggling with housing, unemployment, education, health care and the other challenges of poverty. Philanthropy can incentivize these for-profit investors by paying for enough of the upgrades to make their deals meet their minimum required returns. Less than another 5% of The Giving Pledge funds would allow us deliver clean water to these 21 million Americans. All at the hands of the most experienced management teams in the industry.

All investors, including individuals, pension funds and university endowments, have a large part of their portfolio invested in alternative investments like private equity. They rely on these third-party managers to make direct investments that require hands-on specialized skills over the long-run. They identify opportunities, conduct thorough due diligence, structure and close the investment. These investors rely on these top performing teams to deliver uncorrelated returns for their portfolios to make sure their funds grow. The same skilled approach is available to philanthropists and can be used by corporate philanthropy and others as well. Outsourcing this work to large venture philanthropists is the way forward to deploy The Giving Pledge funds and the larger funds behind them.

The mindset change to invest all the resources needed to reach large-scale impact is the result of a shift in capitalism that I also attribute to The Giving Pledge and to the wealthy millennials that started the asset management revolution towards social impact. Capitalism is no longer just about accumulating nor is it a "winner takes all" game, and just having more is no longer as "cool." Now those with the most wealth and this cutting-edge mindset are looking to solve challenges. This is redefining success to measuring it by what good one can finance, as a result of one's success.

Large venture philanthropy organizations are already creating large deployment vehicles to scale more great nonprofits. This early institutionalization of philanthropy will make it easier to move those funds off the sidelines and into larger impact. Nevertheless, there may be only 50 or 150 nonprofits that can readily take in $200 million to scale their operations. Blue Meridian Partners is showing the way to help philanthropists do this with larger amounts. They are scaling ten nonprofits and deploying over $2 billion over ten years to get them to the next level. Co-Impact, The Audacious Project, and a few other third-party organizations are engaging in this venture philanthropy work at a larger scale.

If we assume that they and new venture philanthropy organizations scale 150 nonprofits in a similar way, with $200 million each, that will represent $30 billion in philanthropy to be deployed over ten years. $30 billion is an enormous amount of philanthropy deployed into a few nonprofits, yet this shockingly represents only 5% of The Giving Pledge funds. The Giving Pledge funds would max-out in the rapidly scalable nonprofit world at 5% of their 2022 estimates.

This may seem daunting but there is good news. The rest can go into PRI at scale so that for-profits can take in the other 95% (and much more) and deliver the large-scale impact and the solutions that our communities deserve. Fortune 500 companies, private equity firms, affordable housing developers all can use more capital to generate impact that is otherwise uneconomical for them. Through PRI, for-profits can receive these funds, structured carefully, to maximize impact instead of merely increasing their profits. There is a long history of blending philanthropy into for-profits to accelerate impact that would otherwise not be generated.

PRI and other philanthropic investments in private deals can be done in much larger amounts to unlock great impact. They have mostly been done at the "venture" level and need to be done at the "later stage" level, to borrow private equity terminology. When it comes to affordable housing, clean energy, clean water and other sectors, the capital needs are enormous. Venture philanthropy at scale can deploy the unused philanthropy and allow these private partners to conduct more business while unlocking immense impact. At the same time, the fullness of joy and immense fulfilment can be delivered to philanthropists and their families. This approach can also unlock further impact by deploying government funds in the same targeted way.

With PRI at scale, we can now fund the solutions to many of our social and environmental challenges that have seemed unsurmountable for so long.

Notes

1. National Alliance to End Homelessness, https://endhomelessness.org/homelessness-in-america/who-experiences-homelessness/children-and-families/.
2. The Wealth-X Billionaire Census 2018, Wealth-X, a part of the Euromoney Institutional Investor PLC Group, https://www.wealthx.com/report/the-wealth-x-billionaire-census-2018/.
3. The Nonprofit Center in Brief 2019, Urban Institute, National Center for Charitable Statistics, June 18, 2020
4. Ford Foundation 2019 Form 990. Ford Foundation, www.fordfoundation.org.
5. The MacArthur Foundation is giving away another $100 million gift and helping others make big bets, Fast Company, February 2, 2019, https://www.fastcompany.com/90312915/the-macarthur-foundation-is-giving-away-another-100-million-gift-and-helping-other-make-big-bets.
6. Early Warning! Why Reading by the End of Third Grade Matters, A KIDS COUNT, Special Report on the Importance of Reading by 3rd Grade, Annie E. Casey Foundation, January 1, 2010, https://www.aecf.org/resources/early-warning-why-reading-by-the-end-of-third-grade-matters/.
7. The 2018 Annual Homeless Assessment Report (AHAR): Part 2, U.S. Department of Housing and Urban Development, HUD Exchange, https://www.hudexchange.info/resource/6161/2018-ahar-part-2-estimates-of-homelessness-in-the-us/.

8. Report on the Economic Well-Being of U.S. Households in 2018, Federal Reserve Board publications, Board of Governors of the Federal Reserve System, Washington, May 2019, https://www.federalreserve.gov/publications/files/2018-report-economic-well-being-us-households-201905.pdf.

9. 21 million Americans don't have access to safe drinking water. That can put them at higher risk of getting COVID-19, Holly Secon and Havovi Cooperjul, Business Insider, July 12, 2020, https://www.businessinsider.in/science/news/21-million-americans-dont-have-access-to-safe-drinking-water-that-can-put-them-at-higher-risk-of-getting-covid-19-/articleshow/76925961.cms.

10. The National Rivers and Streams Assessment 2008/2009, United States Environmental Protection Agency, https://www.epa.gov/sites/production/files/2016-03/documents/fact_sheet_draft_variation_march_2016_revision.pdf.

11. Blue Bonds: An Audacious Plan to Save the World's Oceans. How upfront philanthropy could provide debt relief for island nations and unlock $1.6 billion for ocean conservation, The Nature Conservancy, April 15, 2019, https://www.nature.org/en-us/what-we-do/our-insights/perspectives/an-audacious-plan-to-save-the-worlds-oceans/.

"...what really starts fighting is possessions. And people get into fights by preferring things to people"
— Thomas Merton

2

From PE To PRI

Nabisco had a factory in Palmira, outside of Cali, Colombia. My father ran
the company there and his office was at the factory. It was not uncommon for
the delivery trucks to have to wait for the peacocks who roamed the campus
to get out of the way after fanning their train feathers, so deliveries could
begin. "Such is life in the tropics," he would say. My father was from West-
brook, Maine, and had attended Colby College with help from the G. I. Bill,
before working for U.S. companies overseas all his life.

In contrast, I was born in Cali and grew up there and in Argentina before
heading to Exeter, New Hampshire, for boarding school. It was then that my
father explained to me how Kolhberg, Kravis, & Roberts (KKR & Co. Inc.)
was taking over Nabisco in a leveraged buyout. It was 1989 and this was the
first time I had heard about private equity.

As I read *Barbarians at the Gate: The Fall of RJR Nabisco*, I started trying
to understand what private equity was and what all the accounting, financial and legal terms meant. Then, as a student at Georgetown University, I
spent my junior year abroad, beginning with the summer in São Paulo, fall
semester in Rio de Janeiro, spring semester in Paris and the following summer
in Hong Kong. Georgetown's School of Foreign Service greatly encouraged
international studies.

At the time, my idea of a career was that I would also run U.S. multina-
tionals in Latin America. The ex-patriate life I experienced growing up was
very attractive, as it had provided in many ways an idyllic childhood. In the
fall of 1995, I reached out to several large companies for a summer internship
before my semester started in Rio. I never heard back from companies like

Coca-Cola or Ford or anyone else. I was only able to obtain a summer job in São Paulo with a bank, J. P. Morgan, who hired me to join their Mergers and Acquisitions (M&A) team. It was very different from the manufacturing world I knew, and a nice introduction to finance and to working in a large financial institution. It was also a relatively quiet summer from a work point of view and I really enjoyed seeing the world from this different financial perspective.

Two months later as I began my studies in Rio, a friend asked me if I would like to help his father at a new private equity firm. My friend explained that his father needed someone to write their prospectus in English. That semester I spent three days a week working for International Venture Partners, an early player in private equity in Brazil. It was a great combination of the management and operations work of a multinational and the financial work of an investment bank.

One of the founders, Paul Tierney, invited me into meetings with very senior global finance leaders. His bright, kind and friendly approach showed me what a private equity investor could be like. He had also been in the Peace Corps and was dedicated to many global philanthropic initiatives. Paul was low-profile, a highly successful financier, and had a calling to make good happen. Naturally, Paul became a mentor and someone I would aspire to be.

It turned out that he was teaching in the MBA program at Georgetown when I returned for my senior year, and I was allowed to take his course as an undergraduate. It was fascinating, and Paul advised that if I wanted to enter private equity, I should go to Wall Street for my first job. I took his advice and joined J. P. Morgan in its investment banking training program once I graduated. I started working with their acquisition finance group in power-related businesses and helped some Latin American clients improve their credit rating scores with the large rating agencies.

It was just before my first year was completed with J. P. Morgan in 1998 that I received a call from Patrice Etlin who I knew from International Venture Partners. He had been hired by Advent International to open their office in Brazil and he wanted me to join him as an Associate. At first I declined, as I had not heard of Advent. Fortunately, I was speaking with a friend who had just joined Texas Pacific Group and he explained that Advent was the "real deal." I was fortunate that Patrice had not yet hired anyone, and I started working there a few weeks later. I was part of a small team that was deploying Advent's first fund in Latin America with $250 million in commitments. Patrice was a great mentor and I was also fortunate to spend time with Ernest Bachrach, one of Advent's most admired senior partners, and someone who has continued to provide time to me over the years. Like Paul, Ernest and

Patrice shared the intangibles of many successful traditional private equity executives I had met: down-to-earth, kind, funny, hard-working, earnest, wise and focused on including the opinions and harnessing the enthusiasm of younger team members.

Advent was a lot of fun. It was not uncommon for Advent's partners to have Associates that were being recruited call me. They knew my great enthusiasm for the work would entice them to come on-board. Much like large venture philanthropy is today, private equity in Latin America in 1998 was very new, and few had even heard of it. Much of the work entailed explaining what it was and how it could be beneficial to a family which controlled a large business. It was great work for me as my job was primarily to source deals, manage the due diligence and help our partners close the deals. I built up a group of advisors that could refer deals to us and we had nice deal flow in Brazil.

The job then was very hands on. As we were generalists, I visited with five or so different companies a week, mostly in completely different industries. One might be an insurance company, then a software company, then a food processor, a port operator, a private university, an auto parts distributor and so on. We were looking to deploy our funds into excellent companies with great growth prospects while not overpaying for them. Most of the visits were with the controlling shareholder although sometimes there would be three generations of family members and me. The goal was to quickly determine whether there was an opportunity to make an investment and whether it was worth pursuing.

Making private equity investments in Latin America is not for the faint of heart. In addition to the regular challenges of private equity, we dealt with unreliable courts to settle disputes, the risk of high inflation and currency volatility. Limited Partners made commitments to our fund in U.S. dollars which we converted into local currency to make investments until we grew the companies for a few years and found a buyer or listed their shares in an IPO. Every day that we had the investment was a day when there could be a currency devaluation of say 20%, and all the possible gains in our investments in that country or across Latin America could be lost. If that happened, we would "be cooked!" as Patrice liked to say. It is a testament to the partners that they navigated and continued to excel in those difficult waters with very high returns, fund after fund since that time. Today, Advent is the largest institutional private equity manager in Latin America and one of the largest in the world.

The Advent partners showed me that private equity was an apprenticeship business where visiting and reviewing many companies, and making investments became a trade we had to develop by doing. All we had was our time and so we had to develop views quickly on which companies could work for an investment from our fund. I had to be able to assess all the different aspects of a company and its industry in the first meeting while also building a relationship with the potential sellers. I always enjoyed walking the factory floor with the founder of a company in which we were considering investing in or fully-acquiring, and I have felt similar joy sitting with nonprofit CEOs and hearing about every aspect of their operations.

Usually in the first meeting with the founders, I wanted to gather the key numbers (revenue, growth, net income, cash flow, debt), find out about their competitive situation, their taxes (and how they avoided them), any concentration of suppliers or clients, and any commodity risks to their costs. It was common to have a discussion of how taxes were occasionally not paid, as this was the cheapest source of financing at the time. The fees for not paying your taxes were lower than average interest rates, and it was not a criminal offence. During these discussions, I was getting a sense for the strength of their management team. Could they grow significantly if they were properly funded? Could they improve their operations? Could we add value as investors? It was great that Advent had hundreds of portfolio companies all around the world. It helped us focus on what industries may have similar dynamics in Brazil, and it allowed us to learn the key drivers of that industry before we contacted the owners. It also allowed us to add value pretty quickly. In my work to scale nonprofits, much of this information is publicly available through any nonprofit's Form 990 online.

In Brazil, we mostly tried to purchase all or most of the companies we invested in and there were four ways we could make money: higher growth, higher profitability, "multiple expansion" or by using leverage. First, we could invest in a company that would grow very fast, and then if we sold it in five years, we would be able to sell it for much more. Another way was to increase the profitability of the company. Even if growth was modest, a higher profitability would generate a higher exit price. Third, we could purchase the company for a low multiple of cash flow and sell it for a larger one to get a multiple expansion. This would happen naturally as it grew in size and as we improved the company in various ways, even just by having "institutional" investors like us signalled to the market that it was a strong company. We might have modest growth and increase the profitability marginally but if we bought it for five times cash flow and sold it for nine times, that may be enough to make our fund return goals. Lastly, one could borrow debt to use as leverage which could be paid back by the company and greatly increase our equity value. This could get us to the returns our investors needed to continue to commit to our funds even without growth, increases in profitability or multiple at the time of sale. Unfortunately, Brazil's interest rates were extremely high so leverage was off the table.

Some of the investments we made as a team were companies experiencing turbulence that could be turned around. Scaling nonprofits reminds me of these situations as retooling needs to take place before the company is ready to take on large-scale growth; otherwise, growth itself can be perilous to an organization. Retooling companies is not easy and company culture is an essential aspect of any company, but particularly in nonprofits. Many managers are passionate about the work and most are not adequately compensated. They may have been in their roles for decades, fighting to do the most possible good on a shoestring budget. Just changing their roles or changing the way organizations operate can be very difficult. Systems also may have been abandoned and Band-Aid solutions applied over the years. Transitioning these legacy systems into new, more efficient systems can be a very painful and a long-term challenge.

Turning around a for-profit can be very rewarding and its success can be seen in increases in sales, profitability and cash flow. Increased cash flow can be reinvested to grow the organization so larger cash flow can be attained resulting in a more valuable company. Restructuring private equity firms can be very successful as prices may be low and sometimes great increases in cash flow are possible in the short-run, often by restructuring their liabilities. Nonprofits, however, don't increase cash flow as they grow. They require more cash to grow which is generally raised through donations by companies or individuals and managed by a development team. Due to this, sustainability is hard to achieve as they require constant new donors and major gifts.

A key takeaway for me during my time at Advent was the focus on management. The old adage of the three most important things in private equity investing "management, management, management" was very true in Latin America and I have found it to be very true in large-scale philanthropy today. The other important lesson was that it was hard to make up for paying too high a price for a company.

After Advent, I spent two years with Saratoga Partners, the former private equity arm of Dillon, Read (now UBS). Here I also learned the importance of detailed due diligence, careful planning and supporting management teams to safeguard investments and increase returns. The leveraged-buyouts and restructuring investments we did at the time were interesting and challenging. U.S. private equity was very competitive compared to Brazil as there were already thousands of firms competing to purchase the same companies, which drove company prices very high. The work was more analytical with very limited exposure to company owners, management or their operations, until you reached the final stages of highly-curated acquisition processes run by investment banks.

Just after my first daughter was born, we took a trip to Austria and I went to meet with a friend at a private equity firm in Spain. InvestIndustrial was originally the Benetton family's private equity firm and they were considered a middle market European private equity firm. I thought that Southern Europe would prove to be less competitive than the U.S., that they would have more family-owned businesses, and I knew they had a stable currency, removing that risk from the equation we had investing in Brazil. I was advised to pursue my MBA in Europe if I wanted to join a private equity firm there as all of my experience was in Latin America and the U.S.

I went on to complete my MBA at the London Business School (LBS) and worked for InvestIndustrial in Madrid during the summer of 2003 in between my first and second year in the program. At LBS, I also co-founded the private equity conference (a leading event in private equity to this day) and their private equity institute. I then returned to the U.S. to live in Florida instead of working in private equity in Southern Europe. My eldest daughter was now living in Florida and it proved to me to be more important to be an active father than continue my investment path. I found there was little private equity in 2004 in Florida, and the few there didn't have much of a fit with the international work I had focused on. In terms of finance, Florida had careers mostly in traditional commercial banking and wealth management. I tried the latter and was with Morgan Stanley during the 2008 crisis where we had to convince prospects to open accounts with us as the bank shares were being shorted by investors and clients were pulling their funds while it was being reported on CNN in real time.

It was interesting to see the very limited focus given to philanthropy in wealth management. Everyone wanted to make sure that clients were making their financial targets but there was little time spent on their life targets, especially philanthropy. This was mostly considered something for clients to explore and determine on their own. It was seen as too risky to recommend a nonprofit where a client may have a poor experience, and possibly result in losing a client. And there was an obvious conflict in recommending that clients be more philanthropic because more gifts would lower the assets we managed for clients, and thus our personal income, as much of the compensation was calculated as a percentage of assets. We felt that any discussions about philanthropy were best had between estate attorneys and their clients, as those gifts could play a role on shielding significant assets from taxes, especially estate taxes.

I also learned about using annuities to convert future planned gifts into current major gifts. This gives older donors the opportunity to enjoy a major gift today rather than just be a significant planned giving donor. It can add thousands of prospects to any capital campaign. Jim Larschan from Northwestern Mutual in Palm Beach Garden, showed me how to create this win-win for all, including greater sustainability for nonprofits. Older donors who can't make a major gift because they are on a fixed budget can buy a $250,000 annuity from a nonprofit that pays them, say 6%, for life. Instead, they agree the nonprofit will keep half and pay them 3% instead of 6%. Some donors will welcome the opportunity to make a major gift they can enjoy in life, and forgo some current income. The nonprofit would get about $125,000 immediately, depending on the age of the donor. They can see the impact of their major gift and participate in the celebration of a new program or building rather than only making a gift from their estate when they have passed.

After Morgan Stanley, I decided to focus my time on raising funds for the homeless and I became a development officer for a local nonprofit. While I was raising funds and setting up a major gift and planned giving program, I heard about The Giving Pledge. I realized the signers would have a difficult time fulfilling their pledges. Not because they didn't want to, but because nonprofits had never had the luxury of investing in the type of planning needed to justify very large gifts.

Anyone can give a fortune to endow funds to any school, church, or hospital. These can be critical funds which are at the heart of the financial strength of organizations like The Salvation Army. Giving to create large impact, though, is another matter. I learned first-hand that nonprofits generally do not have any detailed ten-year plans, or the systems to allow them to scale, and therefore lack the ability to give a large donor the sense that they can take in a $50 million gift to scale their organizations.

Here is where my private equity background came together with philanthropy. I realized that the bottleneck created by The Giving Pledge could be resolved by the creation of active managers like Advent International and Texas Pacific Group who can deploy the funds on behalf of donors. Large venture philanthropy firms could create large vehicles to deploy the philanthropy with the same careful process private equity firms rely on for success.

Blue Meridian Partners, Co-Impact and the Audacious Project are leading the way in larger venture philanthropy deployments. Despite each using different terms to describe what they do, the overarching service they provide is value-added help to those looking to make larger gifts. All three have blue-chip philanthropists coming together to fund projects that these large venture philanthropy groups curate for them.

In 2014, I founded Merton, a venture philanthropy firm focused on deploying philanthropy at scale, in order to help solve The Giving Pledge bottleneck and reach solutions. Initially, I had not found anyone doing venture philanthropy with larger funds beyond the existing venture philan-thropy firms (New Profit, Venture Philanthropy Partners, REDF and others) which were operating at the more "venture" level with smaller grants.

At the time, my goal was to create a very compelling growth plan with high impact to greatly scale a leading local nonprofit. This would give large philanthropists an opportunity to make larger gifts. The goal was also to set up a social impact bond model to achieve sustainability at the larger size. This was not a traditional social impact bond funded by private investors looking for a return, in addition to generating impact. This was an attempt to fund the first-ever philanthropic social impact bond, so that cost savings paid by the government would be paid to the nonprofit, rather than exiting the system to pay investors.

What I learned was that in the world of mega-philanthropy, if you build it, they will not necessarily come. I created an $85 million in philanthropy 10-year expansion plan for a leading local nonprofit called Community Partners to increase the number of apartments for formerly homeless individuals from around 80 to 580. We would piggyback on the work that was already being done in Palm Beach County by the Corporation of Supporting Housing in their FUSE program that tracked "frequent users" of the homeless systems. The plan was to house up to 500 of these individuals permanently. This would generate $7 million in annual cost savings to the community in terms of reduced use of the emergency rooms, jails and homeless shelters. The plan then was to sign the first philanthropic social impact bond with the State of Florida to pay back part of those cost savings to help the nonprofit reach sustainability at that larger scale.

The main reason I chose this nonprofit was the quality of its management team in line with my private equity training of prioritizing great manage-ment. Community Partners was run by Patrick McNamara who is widely admired for his management skills and his intense focus on helping those most in need. He was also the only CEO who had heard of Social Impact Bonds at the time and he appreciated the importance of accessing the larger funds that were becoming available. Unfortunately, this nonprofit was mostly grant-funded and we realized that having large funders committed upfront was critical to the success of a large expansion like this. Blue Meridian Partner, Co-Impact and the Audacious Project were created with one or a group of mega-philanthropists from the start.

The presentation I had for this Big Bet expansion was similar to the ones I put together during my finance days earlier in my career. It included a detailed 10-year projection showing the new apartments being added, the new staff and other costs including fundraising and management additions to support the growth. It also showed the income from the philanthropic social impact bond to help attain sustainability at a much larger scale. As I presented the plan to local philanthropists, it was clear that they had not seen anything like it and they were excited by the possibility to have such large and specific impact. At the time, there were about 800 beds for the homeless across various providers and so our project would deliver a 63% increase in the total homeless beds capacity. The first philanthropist I met with surprised me in his reaction. His first reaction was "this may prevent the riots."

I was taken aback by his comment and yet I did understand what he meant. The levels of inequality in the U.S. are reaching unsustainable rates and more and more I'm reminded of the differences in wealth I witnessed living in Colombia, Argentina and Brazil. I believe giving the very wealthy very structured vehicles to outsource mega-gifts in order to relieve social problems can be very beneficial to reduce tensions and reduce suffering. A similar stance was presented by Nick Hanauer in his 2014 TED Talk titled, "Beware, fellow plutocrats, the pitchforks are coming" where he points out the risks of inequality to the wealthy and the need for higher minimum wages.[1] Big Bets are a win-win for all; we need to promote them.

Despite a year of work creating and presenting a plan with great scale and impact, I had to face the fact that very large gifts are mostly made to nonprofits donors have relationships with and a large growth plan is just not enough. Nevertheless, I was on a path to find ways to help solve The Giving Pledge Bottleneck. The fulfilment from doing good at scale can be very rewarding and can drive more to continue to pledge their wealth for good. Giving is an act of service which can transform lives, including that of the donor. Most of the world's religions and spiritual traditions tie helping others with personal fulfilment and realization. The darkness and suffering can be turned into light for both those in need and those doing the helping. As this rising tide of good in the world accelerates, there are many more ways for philanthropists and their families to be more engaged, finance more good and in the process find higher levels of fulfilment.

Note

1. Nick Hanauer, August 12, 2014 TED Talk, "Beware, fellow plutocrats, the pitchforks are coming," https://www.ted.com/talks/nick_hanauer_beware_fellow_plutocrats_the_pitchforks_are_coming?language=en.

"Is there to be found on earth a fullness of joy, or is there no such thing?"
— Thomas Merton, The Way of Chuang Tzu

3

A Rising Tide of Good

There has been a rising tide of good in capitalism. In the last ten to fifteen years, two very significant changes have accelerated this tide. Despite many recent tragedies such as the COVID-19 pandemic and the ongoing suffering in our communities and around the world, a few key individuals within the ranks of the most successful and wealthy took key steps that changed the world's consciousness towards actively and publicly pursing good.

The first is The Giving Pledge which was created by Bill and Melinda Gates and Warren Buffet in 2010. Since its inception, over 200 billionaires have agreed to give the majority of their wealth away during their lifetime or at the end of their life. The spirit of this to me is to inspire others to give large amounts today and to lessen suffering. It is also driven by the increasing desire to see change now and not in 20 years. This is in stark contrast to the way those with the most wealth have traditionally approached philanthropy, where typically they've endowed their wealth in foundations in order to create permanent funding for future causes, and attempting to engage their children and grandchildren in giving to create a legacy. This resulted in smaller gifts available every year in perpetuity.

There are many challenges resulting from the traditional model of philanthropy. Many are controversial and are being looked at and questioned today from an impact point of view by the donor or their family and by the philanthropic community, as well as from a public policy point of view. More than ever, approaches to impact creation are being tested and more are questioning the wisdom of traditional approaches to philanthropy and its existing regulatory frameworks.

© The Author(s), under exclusive license to Springer Nature
Switzerland AG 2021
S. Davis, *Solving the Giving Pledge Bottleneck,*
https://doi.org/10.1007/978-3-030-78865-0_3

Often the original donor wants the foundation to be used as a way for their children and grandchildren to learn how to give back and to absorb values that are important to the donor. Although this does happen, it is also true that new generations are sometimes not interested in the causes their parents and grandparents favoured, and therefore are not active members in their family foundation. Also, the original mission and focus of a foundation can change based on who is on the board. As the board controls all the giving, future gifts will reflect the decisions of the board members and many times these are very different than those favoured by the original donor.

Foundations can play pivotal roles in improving our communities and tackling key social and environmental challenges. Yet given their nature to exist in perpetuity and the resulting limited size of their gifts, it is hard for them to create significant measureable solutions on their own. Many foundations give 5% of their assets every year, which is the minimum required by the IRS. Much larger funds are needed. Coordinating gifts with other foundations is also challenging.

A few foundations were created to, or have decided to "spend down" their endowed funds. The idea is that large funds can be gifted to have a larger impact today and to get us to solve challenges and not just fund incremental impact. Though this trend isn't without controversy, it is growing. There are also calls for higher minimum giving rates by foundations and the establishment of minimum giving rates by Donor Advised Funds (DAFs). During the COVID-19 crisis, various multi-billion dollar foundations (Kellogg, MacArthur and Ford, amongst others) announced that they would be borrowing against their endowed funds to make larger gifts. This is a great start, yet falls short of starting to spend down their funds. This would result in closing their doors once the funds are spent, which is a difficult thing to do. Atlantic Philanthropies has created a model that can be followed in this way.

The Giving Pledge was a strong push to enhance public consciousness towards giving in the moment, to consider spending philanthropic funds rather than endowing them. This movement has inspired many to rethink the role of their wealth and its utility. I think it is also changing capitalism itself. It is shifting the game from, "who has the most," to "who can do the most good," from accumulation and luxury spending to giving and impact. This will have significant consequences as we move forward as a society. We have to thank The Giving Pledge founders for this gift.

It is easy to overlook the impact that over 200 super successful and admired titans of business and finance have had by showing a drastic shift in the focus of what success is. We have yet to see the long-term outcome of these public pledges, but when Elon Musk, Richard Branson, Ray Dalio, Paul Tudor Jones and other highly respected business giants commit to this kind of giving, people listen. There may be cynicism about people's intentions, and it may be deserved in some cases, but I believe the statement of intention, in and of itself, has been very powerful and has shifted the goal of capitalism for the better. If doing good is what these fortunes are being used for and spent in the relative short-term, then what does mean for every other ambitious current and future business leader?

The second significant change that has recently happened in capitalism is how portfolio decisions are made in wealthy families today. Social impact can mean many things, but in the world of asset management, it has meant the movement of investments from traditional companies that offer high returns to companies that offer high returns and also generate some "good." At the outset of this shift, there was more of a focus on not causing harm, but now, there are seemingly endless possibilities to invest for good in the public and private markets and obtain market returns.

Social Impact is commonly defined as investments into publicly traded securities that have been rated according to their positive impact in ESG (Environment, Social, Governance). Social Impact is also considered as investments into private companies (equity and debt) that have a high ESG focus. Yet most refer to Social Impact as those ESG funds invested in public markets. These crossed the $30 trillion mark in 2018 and are growing.[1]

The term "impact investing" will soon be redundant as all investing is evolving to be seen for its social and environmental impact in addition to its financial return. Here, we have to thank very wealthy millennials who initiated this movement by pushing their families and their bankers to divest from their portfolio companies that were polluting, or engaging in many other ills.

Their leadership changed all of wealth management as today no financial advisor can risk not offering ESG investments to their clients. In addition, all global corporations have become keenly focused on being considered a corporation that is highly regarded from an ESG lens. They cannot afford to lose investor interest in their shares if they are known to have negative impacts on the world. Publicly traded companies can no longer risk being perceived as anything but generating good, or attempting to generate good, and being good stewards of their communities. Otherwise, demand for their products and services, and for their shares could plummet.

Although ESG investing has always been around in different forms, it has gained mainstream attention recently. Going back in history we can see how values have been used to influence business decisions. Recent examples are the boycotting of South African goods in the 1980s to pressure South Africa to end Apartheid, resulted in the freeing of Nelson Mandela in 1990, as well as reversing Apartheid and multi-racial elections a few years later. The boycotting of consumer products to cause change in corporate policy, the Fair Trade movement and the Corporate Social Responsibility (CSR) movement have also been examples of advocating for good in capitalism. Corporations today have a need to focus on the impact of their operations on the different communities they operate in. Every corporation has a different approach, just like every individual donor and every foundation have different ways of approaching their impact.

Corporations have philanthropy programs to make grants to local communities. These are limited in scale by their limited size as well as by the ability of nonprofits to present larger detailed and compelling long-term plans. Most grants from foundations, corporations and individuals tend to be one-year grants rather than multi-year ones that allow nonprofits to grow programs over time. Volunteer programs are another way to contribute towards good because of the benefit of engaging employees in causes that may prove important to them and can make for great team-building experiences. Diversity, inclusion and equality are also key ways corporations can have an impact. These can be very measurable, such as the composition of senior management and their Board of Directors. Many have found that increasing impact in their supply chain is the most important alignment they can do.

According to its 2019 Business and Sustainability Report, Coca-Cola is moving its supply chain to fully recycle, source sustainably and produce according to their highest ethical standards.[1] They are also measuring their greenhouse gas (GHG) emissions or carbon footprint, the sustainability of the farming in their supply chain, their responsible water usage and other initiatives according to specific goals. One of their goals is to make all of their packaging 100% recyclable by 2025. Social impact changes in their supply chain are very powerful as they can be measured and implemented across the world. They are fostering impact across their global platform of 225 bottler partners and their 900 bottling plants.[1]

The Coca-Cola Company is rated AAA by the MSCI (Morgan Stanley Capital International) ESG ratings.[1] They are respected for both their corporate governance and sustainability governance in addition to their impact results. Additional ways they create impact is in their relationships with suppliers, consumers, investors, the media, governments and NGOs in their advocacy work to further impact in terms of reducing sugar intake, promoting human rights and others. These are all carefully aligned with their operations and values. They also gifted $125 million to 294 organizations in 129 countries from both their corporate foundation and from their own corporation. Nevertheless, this was only 1.3% of operating income and 0.3% of total revenues.[1]

The #MeToo movement that began in 2017 and accelerated justice for victims of sexual abuse and harassment, the social justice marches and Black Lives Matter movement of 2020, and the U.S. Capitol attack on January 6, 2021, were followed by fast and important announcements and some visible changes by many corporations. They committed to making internal changes, investing in improvements and even withdrawing specific political funding, all in pursuit of being part of positive changes in society by focusing on ESG values and outcomes. Corporations like Patagonia and Nike have, of course, been doing this for decades and it is part of their corporate identity.

Unlike traditional credit ratings from Standard & Poor's and Moody's, or equity research ratings on publicly traded shares, ESG ratings are more subjective yet quickly evolving. There are many ways companies can try to portray their ESG focus. Whether they are publicly traded corporations or private equity firms, most are looking to list their achievements in helping their communities. It is hard to objectively measure impact and compare to the impact of peers, unlike traditional credit ratios which have standard financial metrics that can be applied across all companies in an industry or across the whole economy. One way companies are trying to classify their impact is to look at their operations and see which of the United Nations' 17 Sustainable Development Goals (SDG) fit.

ESG ratings are not new. Metrics in benchmarks and scorecards continue to be developed to quantify the good and well-being on society that a company is generating and help investors see risks associated with not pursuing more aggressive ESG strategies. Impact and ESG frameworks are now central to all corporate and investing activities.[2] According to the Governance and Accountability Institute, a New York-based consulting group, 20% of the S&P 500 companies were publishing a sustainability report in 2011. In 2019, it was 90%.[3] Financial giants are also looking at their operations to generate ESG results. BNP Paribas mandated that 20% of the variable compensation of 7,000 of its employees would be tied to 9 CSR performance indicators. Also, 30 of the largest asset managers, including UBS, have signed up to the Net Zero Asset Management Initiative which looks to reduce carbon emissions across its portfolios.[4]

As wealthy millennials succeeded in pushing for change, they also changed the asset management business as a whole. Now, every bank or asset management company has started efforts or bought firms that rank companies by ESG ratings. They are now offering these to all their clients. As we move forward, social impact will just be one of the necessary criteria in evaluating any investment (public or private). In private equity, firms are being created to invest exclusively in companies that generate a great profit but also do good. Texas Pacific Group's, The Rise Fund, now with $4 billion under management,[5] is the most visible example. Bain Capital Double Impact is also a leader in this space.

Private equity is also shifting and starting to look at scaling good. They are adding ESG metrics in addition to reporting their financial returns. The

Internal Rate of Return (IRR) of a private equity investment is the ultimate and traditional measure of success for that industry, as well as for any investing, including those of other large pools of capital such as hedge funds. New measures or returns will be developed in terms of measurable social and environmental returns. Impact investors looking to use their funds to generate a good will be offered new ways to do that and to more clearly view investment decisions based on a broader set of criteria. Each individual investor or each institution will have to determine that criteria, and that will have profound effects on what are attractive investments and which are not. We will also continue to blend all types of capital, including philanthropy, into mainstream for-profit impact investing.

Two recent announcements exemplify the acceleration of these changes. They themselves are high water marks of the rising tide of good. The first is the announcement by 181 CEOs of the largest corporations in the U.S. that shareholder value is no longer their main goal and that all stakeholders are important. This is a dramatic shift from the existing status quo that CEOs must always maximize shareholder value against all else. This announcement was made on August 19, 2019, at The Business Roundtable meeting.[6]

The other announcement that exemplified the acceleration of these changes was made by BlackRock on January 14, 2020. It stated that all of their investments were now going to be evaluated from a sustainability and climate risk perspective, giving the immediate risk of environmental impact. This is important in many ways, including that BlackRock is the largest asset management company in the world. Making all of their investments have an impact focus better gets to the goal of combining a high financial return with a high ESG rated impact.[7]

These two official announcements were significant and will have effects in the rising tide of good. As we move forward, companies are now motivated to find new ways to do and measure good. Many large and small corporations are also looking at their global supply chains to see how changes in their main operating practices can create good and be tied to one of the 17 UN SDGs Goals. Social impact asset management firms have for many years developed baskets of high ESG rated companies to offer investors. Many of these firms have been purchased by more mainstream banks and wealth management firms. A key acquisition was the purchase of Imprint, considered the top impact investing asset management company, by Goldman Sachs in 2015.[8]

The rising tide of good will continue as ESG investing becomes more mainstream. Everyone, including small companies, are looking to show their impact including the composition of their management teams and their boards in terms in diversity, inclusion and equality. These are very visible ways to compare publicly traded companies, but as you move to their operations and then their overall community impact, they are harder to quantify.

Few, if any, have developed full detailed plans to reach any of the UN SDG goals.

The next stage of impact investing and social impact is setting the course to actually solve our most pressing social and environmental challenges. Creating detailed plans to measure what is needed and determining how to finance the solutions are coming. We have the planning capabilities and the entire set of corporations, nonprofits, investors and governments to execute on this good. The Giving Pledge and the millennials pushing for social impact investments in their portfolios have sparked and begun to fund this type of good.

In this book, I'm advocating for blending The Giving Pledge and other large philanthropy into for-profits at large scale, as this capital will give them the flexibility to unlock massive impact. The philanthropy will allow them to generate this impact economically within their core businesses. This will in turn help philanthropists meet their giving goals and also generate great fulfilment for them and their families, as they see the visible progress. We need to continue to align the incentives of corporations, pension funds, private equity funds, nonprofits and governments with an ESG lens.

This rising tide brings good to all.

Notes

1. The Coca-Cola Company, 2019 Business and Sustainability Report, https://www.coca-colacompany.com/reports/business-sustainability-report-2019.
2. Global Sustainable Alliance Report 2018, Global Sustainable Investment Review.
3. 2020 S&P 500 Flash Report, Governance & Accountability Institute (G&A). https://www.ga-institute.com/research-reports/flash-reports/2020-sp-500-flash-report.html.
4. ESG Investing Came Of Age In 2020 - Millennials Will Continue To Drive It In 2021, Forbes, Chuka Umunna, December 18, 2020 https://www.forbes.com/sites/chukaumunna/2020/12/18/esg-investing-came-of-age-in-2020millennials-will-continue-to-drive-it-in-2021/?sh=247be5409adb.
5. TPG's The Rise Fund website, April 14, 2020, www.therisefund.com.
6. "Business Roundtable Redefines the Purpose of a Corporation to Promote 'An Economy That Serves All Americans' www.businessroundtable.org, August, 19, 2019.
7. "Sustainability as BlackRock's New Standard for Investing." Letter to Clients January 14, 2020. www.blackrock.com.
8. "Goldman Sachs Agrees to Buy Asset Manager Imprint Capital," Michael J. Moore, July 13, 2015, www.bloomberg.com.

"The shadows fall. The stars appear. The birds begin to sleep. Night embraces the silent half of the earth. A vagrant, a destitute wanderer with dusty feet, finds his way down a new road. A homeless God, lost in the night, without papers, without identification, without even a number, a frail expendable exile lies down in desolation under the sweet stars of the world and entrusts Himself to sleep."
— Thomas Merton

4

A Failure in Planning

In 2015, I had set up a major gifts and planned giving program at a nonprofit fighting homelessness in Florida. The complexities of the challenges associated with the massive suffering across every city in America due to homelessness are quite staggering. There was also a vast array for nonprofits, private and government services tackling parts of the system. The data was not clear and planning was limited due to limited funds and resources.

Leading nonprofits can have dedicated and talented management and still have to make choices of whether to serve more people suffering today or invest in planning and systems to have better data and reporting for donors. On my first day in 2010, our CEO told me there was a 10-year plan to end homelessness for our county, and so my work would be "cut-out for me." The plan had been published two years prior in 2008.

Out of habit, when I printed the report I went to the back to see the numbers first. I had been trained at J. P. Morgan to look at the financials first in analysing companies to get a sense of size, scope, growth and profitability, amongst other things. It would quickly give me a picture of the company being analysed, its financial and strategic health and trajectory. It would also generate the first questions to be asked to assess the company and its industry dynamics.

I was not prepared for what I found. It is still hard to understand unless you spend significant time in the nonprofit world. I was confused as the county's report had virtually no numbers. Instead, there was a Zagat's dining guide type system.[1] It showed a list of all the items needing funding and next to it was "$" to "$$$$" depending on the need. I later realized the lack of

S. Davis, *Solving the Giving Pledge Bottleneck*,
https://doi.org/10.1007/978-3-030-78865-0_4

detailed planning and the lack of projections in the nonprofit world was a global problem.

As I write this book, I'm reviewing again their Ten-Year Plan To End Homelessness, and I appreciate how useful and thorough it is on the many aspects of homelessness in Palm Beach County, here in Florida. It gives historical, political, economic context, details the various providers of homeless services, what services they each focus on, the various challenges facing them, the complex group of services needed to help the different types of homeless populations, and in summary, it offers great qualitative information. It was developed over a two-year period according to national norms by a group of local leaders involved in the homeless arena, and it was a great step forward from not having a qualitative plan of this magnitude. It also has been a document to guide the county government and nonprofit leaders in moving forward in more of a concerted effort. What is missing, however, is the detailed financial plan showing the exact costs needed, how those will be paid for and who will execute on the housing and services at a larger scale.

The general understanding was that increased tax revenue would be the way to fund all the homeless needs. At the same time, it was understood that there was no political appetite for that. Most of the homeless services providers were operating with very tight budgets, and it was difficult to justify investments in fundraising teams in order to raise more funds. So the need persisted and continues to persist today. This is a national issue that was highlighted well for me as tied to Dan Pallota's Overhead Myth[2] on the one hand and on the limited tax funds on the other. Ironically, there is significant evidence that the cost savings of housing the homeless and providing the services needed would generate cost savings that would cover the additional spending. Much of the Social Impact Bond work has already been demonstrated in several pilot programs for each.

It has been incredible to see the teams of homeless providers show up every day to face the daily unending waves of homeless needing food, clothes, medicine, medical care, funds for motels, jobs, education and housing. Housing is very capital intensive and it is the core piece to give stability to individuals and families so that they can have an opportunity to address their other challenges. Funds for motels are limited, run out and as shelters and other housing are always full, the management teams and staff of these nonprofits do what they can to help. But many times it is just to listen, try to console and ask them to come back the next day. It was very fulfilling for me to see the success of a few who entered our housing, maybe started taking medication and became stable and were able to work and secure their own apartment. They went from chronically homeless to just like any member of our staff. Some joined our staff and you would not be able to tell who was formerly homeless and who was not. It was truly transformative work. I sometimes have people take me aside in a conference or students I teach tell me in class that they were homeless at one point. I would not be able to tell them apart from their current colleagues. Disaster hits us anytime in different ways. Help from friends and family is not always there.

At the same time, I read our nonprofit's strategic plan. Like the county's plan, this one too had very few numbers. There were no financial projections and most slides were qualitative descriptions and aspirational goals. Its use was to have high-level discussions on the vision and mission of the organization, but it was not a management tool, or a plan that would be used in the for-profit world. This plan also didn't chart a long-term course detailing specific investments needed in people, systems, real estate nor a detailed plan of where we would obtain the funds to do so. It also did not specify how we would be more sustainable through new sources of revenue or by having more endowed funds.

This was not a unique challenge. I have yet to come across a nonprofit that has a detailed plan on paper to solve the issue it was created to solve. I have seen a few plans to scale a nonprofit with $100 or 200 million, and I have created 3 similar plans, but only one was to solve the entire challenge for a geographic area. This planning challenge is endemic to the nonprofit world. Strategic plans in the nonprofit world are neither strategic, nor are they plans, from a for-profit point of view. And how could they be when we penalize nonprofits from investing in planning and strategy work?

In 2010, I also join the Board of Directors of the Palm Beach County affiliate of the National Alliance on Mental Illness. After 30 years with a $30,000 a year budget and no staff, we started writing some grants and attracting more donors. Within 5 years, we had grown revenue to over $600,000 and had 8 staff. It was still a small fraction of the work that was needed but significant growth was possible. Planning was still hard to develop as most of the resources were devoted to running the day-to-day and few grants made allowances for much "overhead" including planning and strategy work.

One year we had a day-long retreat to develop its strategic plan with an outside expert. After a day of qualitative exercises where we discussed the programs to prioritize and which events to develop, we ended the session. We also had interesting discussions about the mission and vision of the organization. I asked the expert if we were now going to assign numbers to these initiatives and create a financial plan and wondered if we planned to do that the next day, and I was just unaware of it. I was told that the plan was done. Again, no numbers.

Culturally, the nonprofit world management teams, as far as I have seen, do not have the skilled training in financial planning beyond budgeting for the current year. Current year budgets can already be complex as grant requirements for spending and reporting can be overwhelming, especially for any federal grants. Smaller nonprofits can easily get overwhelmed by funder requirements. To make things worse, grants tend to be very short-term, mostly just one year, and have the onerous grant management costs every year. Therefore, the idea of designing sophisticated plans for sophisticated philanthropists is not a rational proposition in traditional philanthropy. Of course, this is all changing with The Giving Pledge.

Vox reported in June of 2020 that Jack Dorsey was going to be quickly giving away $1 billion[3] with similar lack or strings attached and paperwork as MacKenzie Scott has managed to do. It reports that he has given $90 million away but recently he has surpassed $400 million in giving. Elon Musk, who signed The Giving Pledge when he was worth $2 billion[4] and is now worth close to $200 billion,[5] may also come up with a new accelerated method to generate impact and solve our greatest challenges. Just his asset growth may cause revisions in the estimated total amount theoretically available in Giving Pledge commitments to inch closer to $1 trillion. The article also mentions that Jack Dorsey's approach may be in part to break out of the crit-icisms emerging against billionaire philanthropy as the best path for change. It references Anand Giridharadas who has been a vocal critique of billionaires for assuming they can solve the world problems. He rose to celebrity status in the giving world with his 2018 book Winners Take All: The Elite Charade of Changing the World following his famous Aspen Institute speech in 2015.[6] We shall see what innovations emerge for large-scale solutions by these and other individuals.

I believe leveraging for-profits to do more good by blending philanthropy into their projects is the way forward. Having nonprofit Big Bets take-in $1 trillion (not quite so much yet) is challenging. These funds can be blended into large for-profits to unlock great impact and can also encourage govern-ments to fund even larger amounts for solutions through for-profit later stage companies. It's a question of managing the deployment and executing on the work to deploy the funds. We need management teams that can take in enor-mous funds in later stage companies, many in capital-intensive industries that also happen to be able to generate much higher additional good with the flexibility philanthropy provides. We are looking at leveraging for-profits in affordable housing, water infrastructure, clean water and others, which have the deals to take in larger funds and have the management teams with the track record to put them to work. Naturally, this also reduces the risk of the philanthropy while funding projects that are sustainable already (as these are for-profits) and increasingly more sustainable at larger levels.

Dan Pallota's popular Ted Talk in 2013[2] has been viewed almost 5 million times and wonderfully explains the root causes of how nonprofits cannot take more than a portion of these funds for specific solutions as they have been consistently starved for management resources. We expect nonprofits to operate on a shoestring budget and punish them for investing in management compensation, systems, marketing and by taking risks in new ways to fundraise like providing great customer experiences for donors. They are gauged and considered poorly managed, and suspect, if their overhead ratio goes too far past 20% without any consideration for their impact and their growth. The solution to this is to evaluate nonprofits based on their growth plans, the increases in measurable impact and their trajectory towards solving the challenge they are looking to solve. Taking a snapshot of costs as a percentage of total revenue does not reflect the quality or scope of their impact. But in a world where we punish them from being able to invest in great impact measuring and reporting tools, it is hard to point to other data that can be comparable across nonprofit sectors.

The lack of planning and detailed projections in the Ten-Year Plan To End Homelessness were both shocking and mystifying to me. How could a plan have no numbers? The qualitative part of the plan was very good, but how can this be useful without a detailed financial projection quantifying all the needs described, let alone all quantifying the resources needed to solve the problem.

When choices need to be made between housing a mother with two kids who is living in her car, even if just in a motel for a few nights, or setting aside funds to create detailed plans, the latter loses importance in the moment. Given overwhelming need every day, the planning to justify a $200 million gift to have impact in an area just doesn't happen. Yet without the plans showing the impact, how can we attract the funds needed at the level necessary?

I was part of many meetings with the homeless services providers in our region, and I have found a similar dynamic across the country and throughout other causes such as education, health care, community development and others. We met regularly and the message always was: "if only we work better together we can solve this problem." The issue was not better collaboration amongst providers, although that can help on the margin, relative to the size of the entire challenge at a county level. The funds they all raised were still a small fraction of what a detailed 10-year plan would call for annually. So the answer is simple, we have to grow that pie.

Every year, about 3 gifts a season were reported in the Palm Beach Daily News of $50 million and above. This is "the island" of Palm Beach which has the formal name as the Town of Palm Beach. These gifts were mostly from part-time residents who came to Palm Beach County for the season roughly between Christmas and Labour Day. All the gifts were always to well-known nonprofits in New York, Boston or Chicago, where they had their main residences. The reports regularly caused indignation amongst the CEOs of the homeless services nonprofits for these gifts were not being given to them. Why did these part-time residents not come to them with these types of funds to help them? It was a logical question, but it revealed more about the lack of investing in planning than the intent of donors. None of these providers had presentations that could be shown to these residents with clear and detailed plans justifying a $50 million gift in any way. They also had very little access to be able to present them the plans.

Naturally, these donors have long-standing ties with the nonprofits they give this large philanthropy to. These nonprofits have also been asking for these gifts and developing personal relationships and engaging the donors and their families in meaningful ways with seasoned major gifts officers for decades. They also have well-developed capital campaign consultants and presentations detailing the cost of a building or program they would like funded. Although schools and universities, churches, museums and hospitals dominate the major gifts realm of giving, social services and others helping the poor are starting to get larger gifts.

While naming buildings is nice, there is a growing demand for larger gifts which have greater measurable impact and "move the needle" on issues like social justice and equity. Scaling nonprofits can somewhat solve many issues, at least locally. These gifts require detailed 10-year plans showing the growth and conveying the management strength and competency to deliver that growth. We simply are not asking for $100 million gifts because nonprofits across the world do not have detailed presentations that make a strong case for the support.

Fortunately, the funds are there, waiting. They are starting to come in even without the plans as seen in 2020 and 2021 with MacKenzie Scott's gifts. More plans should yield more gifts. Yet as Elon Musk tweeted recently "Btw, critical feedback is always super appreciated, as well as ways to donate money that really make a difference (way harder than it seems)."[7]

Notes

1. Ten-Year Plan To End Homelessness in Palm Beach County, September 23, 2008, https://discover.pbcgov.org/communityservices/PDF/HomelessAdvisory/ten-year-plan.pdf.
2. Dan Pallota, TED Talks, The way we think about charity is dead wrong, March 11, 2013, https://www.ted.com/talks/dan_pallotta_the_way_we_think_about_charity_is_dead_wrong.
3. What you should know about Jack Dorsey's surprising $1 billion commitment to charity, Theodore Schleifer, Vox, April 7, 2020, https://www.vox.com/recode/2020/4/7/21212757/coronavirus-jack-dorsey-charity-billion-llc.
4. Elon Musk Has Promised To Give At Least Half His Fortune To Charity. Here's How Much He's Donated So Far, Hayley C. Cuccinello, Forbes, September 8, 2020, https://www.forbes.com/sites/hayleycuccinello/2020/09/08/elon-musk-has-promised-to-give-at-least-half-his-fortune-to-charity-heres-how-much-hes-donated-so-far/?sh=2a11a2b83c8c.
5. Elon Musk is once again the world's richest person as he and Jeff Bezos keep jockeying for the lead, Tim Levin, Business Insider, February 19, 2021. https://www.businessinsider.com/elon-musk-jeff-bezos-net-worth-worlds-richest-tesla-amazon-stock-2021-1#:~:text=Elon%20Musk%20is%20once%20again,keep%20jockeying%20for%20the%20lead&text=Elon%20Musk%20became%20the%20world's,net%20worth%20is%20%24194%20billion.
6. Anand Giridharadas on elite do-gooding: 'Many of my friends are drunk on dangerous BS', Lucia Graves, *The Guardian*, December 18, 2018, https://www.theguardian.com/us-news/2018/dec/18/anand-giridharadas-author-aspen-wealthy-elite.
7. Elon Musk Tweet. January 7, 2021.

But if you want to identify me, ask me not where I live, or what I like to eat, or how I comb my hair, but ask me what I think I am living for, in detail, and ask me what I think is keeping me from living fully for the thing I want to live for. Between these two answers you can determine the identity of any person
—Thomas Merton

5

The Giving Pledge Bottleneck

Houston we have a problem.

In 2016, I was teaching a group of Austrian MBAs who were studying at Palm Beach Atlantic University for part of the summer. I had a week-long class the business school had asked me to co-teach with Jeremy Morse, a nonprofit CEO, on social impact and nonprofit management. I was giving an overview of the local homeless challenge and how there were 800 beds available across all the local nonprofits to house about 5,000 homeless. The official number was lower as the "Point-In-Count" system was based on volunteers going out on one day, every other year, and physically counting the homeless they could find. They used about 200 volunteers to cover a county of 1.5 million and didn't include many such as those who were homeless or staying with family or friends. The Point-In-Count is conducted every other year as required to obtain certain HUD funding. It reported 1,607 homeless in 2017.[1] Yet the local school district alone reported 3,347 children homeless that year in Palm Beach County.[1] This also reflected the national, system-wide lack of funding, even in basic data. I estimated there being closer to 5,000 homeless in the county.

When I explained this and reiterated that the total number of beds available for our whole region was a fraction of the families and individuals that are homeless, there was much silence. Then, I explained innovations such as Social Impact Bonds in this space and that was met with more silence. Finally, one of the students asked, "why don't you just raise taxes and house everyone in need?" I had to explain that we didn't like to raise taxes especially in this environment, even though taking care of the homeless challenge actually saves us money as a country. This is similar to many of our other social and environmental challenges. Many can recall cases of government spending that was wasted or not optimal, and that makes using tax funds to solve very efficient and effective government solutions politically impossible. This is an important reason why we underinvest in everything from education, to homeless housing, to water infrastructure. The students could not believe this. We discussed how the solution here is to have philanthropy lead the way to show success and then have more private and government funds follow.

Back in 2012, I had started following The Giving Pledge. This seemed to potentially be a significant pool of funds to do just this. Bill and Melinda Gates and Warren Buffet were inspiring many of the most successful individuals in the world to publicly pledge to give much more and sooner. Today, the pool of funds over 200 signers may give away has grown to a significant amount due to their continued success as entrepreneurs and business leaders and to the increases in the public markets. We can finance the solutions of many of our local and global challenges with these funds if they were deployed in targeted large-scale ways. The philanthropy itself can be transformative, and even more importantly, it can scale solutions that can then catalyse more individual and corporate philanthropy, social impact investments, as well as more government funds. It is estimated that The Giving Pledge funds are approaching $600 billion in pledges.[2] Given recent increases in wealth, especially with Elon Musk and the increases in the market capitalization of companies like Amazon, we could say these numbers may be approaching $1 trillion. And this from just over 200 of the over 2,825 billionaires in the world in 2019 as reported by Wealth-X in their Billionaire Census 2020.[3]

The signing of The Giving Pledge is a public statement that signers have the intent to give half or more of their wealth while they are alive or at death. Most have published a letter on The Giving Pledge website and these pledges are not legal commitments, and they are not funds sitting in an account somewhere. The commitments are still part of the wealth holdings of each signer. They are not all looking to actively quantify and determine how they will meet their pledge but it is a statement meant to inspire others and for many, something to be worked on in the future. Nevertheless, this initiative is a significant development as these signers are committing publicly to take action. This means the funds to solve many of our social and environmental challenges are now available, especially when used to attract additional types of funds.

The challenge of course is how to encourage these signers to actually start giving these funds away in meaningful amounts and into solutions.

Recently, more questions are being asked about whether the signers are actually intending on giving their funds away. There has been a public backlash against DAFs and foundations not giving away enough of the funds they hold. Will there be a public backlash against The Giving Pledge? Why are larger gifts not happening?

The Bill and Melinda Gates Foundation, which manages The Giving Pledge, is taking steps to encourage the creation of larger giving opportunities and the giving or larger amounts. On January 23, 2021, Mark Harris wrote a piece in GeekWire called "Gates Foundation gives millions to help persuade ultra-wealthy donors to give more of their billions.[4]" He mentions they gave $5 million to the TED Foundation's Audacious Project in 2020 and the MacArthur Foundation's Lever For Change a similar amount in 2019 to "overcome barriers to large scale giving" by the ultra-wealthy. We have to develop more vehicles to attract and deploy the funds.

Given my background in both private equity and nonprofit management, I realized back in 2012 that there was going to be a problem. I could see a massive bottleneck coming as nonprofits were limited in their ability to effectively present a case to raise the enormous funds needed, given their lack of large detailed plans at scale to justify the mega-gifts, let alone the ability to prove their ability to execute on such ground-breaking scale. This has proven to be the case. It has been reported that giving rates by the signers of The Giving Pledge have been miniscule relative to their pledges. They are smaller still in terms of having impact as much of the giving that has take place, has been to a family's own foundation and not to solve challenges today as originally intended.

Even those who have lead in giving are not on track to give most of their wealth away. Michael Bloomberg has been incredibly philanthropic, giving almost $10 billion away since signing The Giving Pledge in 2010. Yet with a net worth reported by MarketWatch at $54.9 billion in 2020, he may need to give $7–8 billion a year to meet his goal.[5] There are significant exceptions to this, such as the founders of The Giving Pledge and such as Charles Feeney, who has given away over $8 billion through his Atlantic Philanthropies. This represents almost 100% of his wealth.[6]

MacKenzie Scott has created a new path many may be well served to follow. She is committing funds to groups like Blue Meridian Partners who are looking to help scale nonprofits and she is also giving very significant amounts in large unrestricted gifts to organizations she has never met. Thomas Merton, the renowned spiritual writer and Cistercian monk, talked of a meeting with zen master D. T. Suzuki at Columbia University in 1964, where Merton graduated from. They were in a tea ceremony and master Suzuki took an unexpected huge and fast gulp of his tea once they were alone.[7] Merton said it was as if the roof had been blown of the house!

MacKenzie Scott's huge and fast giving has blown off the roof of the world of philanthropy. She gave over $8 billion in unrestricted gifts in 2020 and 2021 to organizations not well known to her. This is ground-breaking.[8] Money needs to flow to these organizations which are leaders in the fights for greater equality, diversity and gender rights, amongst others. If each nonprofit she and her advisors selected doesn't have a detailed plan to scale with say, $100 million of her money, is she supposed to help them create these plans? How long would that take and who would help them do that? On the other hand, if they don't have the long-term plans to quantify and show exactly how they will solve their cause or move them forward significantly, how efficient will they be?

My guess is that something had to give. She couldn't wait for all the planning, although she is supporting that approach as well with Blue Meridian and others like it. The aggressive increase in her wealth makes even the almost $8 billion she gave away (that we know about) be less than what here assets probably increased those years. So there is urgency for much larger giving by the signers of The Giving Pledge to stay ahead of their increases in assets. Nevertheless, there are limited paths to do so without handing vast gifts without a clear path to a solution, beyond just trusting them to continue to do what they are doing. More importantly though, a lack of a large detailed growth plan means these organizations may still not be able to invest more management resources needed to get to a larger solution. They may still be under the restrictions of their overhead ratio despite having a one-time transformative gift. What we need for more scale is more management skills around managing scale.

On June 4, 2015, Brendan Coffey wrote an article on www.Bloomberg.com titled, "Pledge Aside, Dead Billionaires Don't Have to Give Away Half Their Fortune." In it, he reported that 10 signers of The Giving Pledge had already passed away and seemingly not given half their money away.[9] Has this trend continued in the 6 years since then? His article made me wonder why this was happening and how were the signers being held accountable. How is their giving being tracked to in fact celebrate they attaining their pledge? This is difficult of course as the wealth of signers is not all publicly available and all their giving isn't either. When I discuss the issue, it is met with cynicism. The reaction is often one of contempt for the signers for not following through on their pledges. The accumulation of philanthropic funds within Donor Advised Funds can lead one to have a similar initial reaction. There were $142 billion held by DAFs in 2019 that had not yet reached the nonprofits that can help those suffering today.[10] Having contempt for either of these though I believe is misguided. In the case of the latter, contributions to DAFs reached $39 billion yet grants from DAFs were a healthy $27 billion in the same year (a 15% jump from the previous year).

On April 26, 2016, the Journal of Wealth Management published an article I co-authored with Paul G. Schervish, Richard L. Cosnotti and Kirby S. Rosplock, called Solving The Giving Pledge Bottleneck.[11] We had been discussing innovations at the intersection of private equity and philanthropy to scale giving and solve large challenges in our communities and around the world. They had joined my Advisory Board at Merton Capital Partners and we authored this piece to share our ideas.

The Giving Pledge suffers from a significant bottleneck, as donors are not being offered places to allocate $100 million or $1 billion in a way they can be certain will generate the high impact they would want. They also are just starting to learn that they can outsource this whole process to large venture philanthropy firms like Blue Meridian Partners, Co-Impact and The Audacious Project. Many Ultra High Net Worth Individuals may not know this. These organizations too may refer to themselves as "collaborative philanthropy" or "capital aggregation" but for the purposes of this book, I see them as engaging in large third-party venture philanthropy advisory work and deploying funds on behalf of mega-donors. They are "active managers."

It is supremely difficult to give large gifts to organizations that cannot deliver a compelling and detailed 10-year plan. How can you allocate $100 million to a cause without having certainty that the organization itself is sound from a financial point of view? That they have a clear and detailed plan on how the funds need to be spent, that they have articulated and quantified the risks and developed sound strategies to mitigate these risks? How can they trust that a nonprofit management team which has managed a 3% annual growth rate to run an organization that will be 5 times larger or grow at 25% a year? Can they show a detailed plan to scale their systems in a credible way? Has their accounting and legal work been audited to ensure there is not a terrible surprise waiting?

These are just some of the questions a private equity investment requires, and large venture philanthropy deployments require too. These questions are already being asked in large multi-year giving at scale. Venture philanthropy firms have operated successfully making about $100,000 to $3 million grants to smaller innovative nonprofits. The early leaders including New Profit of Boston, Venture Philanthropy Partners of Washington, D.C., and REDF of San Francisco, have each deployed well over $80 million over the last 20 years (some significantly more).[12] Like private equity firms, these organizations are third-party active managers, deploying capital to grow organizations. REDF is most directly affiliated with private equity as its founder, George Roberts, is one of the founders of KKR. As stated in their website, "Using the principles he developed while leading KKR, the global private equity investment firm he co-founded, Roberts structured REDF to undertake venture philanthropy, with the mindset of an investor, and an expected return measured in people with jobs and lives changed.[13]"

As Giving Pledge signers begin to focus on meeting their pledges, many are coming together to deploy larger funds. Large venture philanthropy organizations are emerging. These are organizations that donors can outsource their philanthropic investing to and who provided long-term value-added support to the nonprofits they are helping to grow.

These third-party organizations are designed to provide long-term financial support and similar management assistance to help significantly grow nonprofits at a larger scale. Blue Meridian Partners in New York is deploying up to $200 million in philanthropy into about 10 nonprofits over 10 years, on behalf of donors. Before agreeing to make one of its "Big Bets" into a nonprofit, they first work directly with the management team of that nonprofit and carefully build a 5- or 10-year plan showing exactly what the funds will do and the impact gained in scaling at this great level. Bridgespan, a leading nonprofit consulting company, is assisting in this ground-breaking and necessary planning process. Blue Meridian also goes inside the nonprofit to conduct extensive due diligence to have great certainty that their donor funds are safe. This is made easier in that they have a unique history as being incubated at the Edna McConnell Clark Foundation that was already supporting many of these nonprofits.

In order to solve The Giving Pledge Bottleneck, we need more vehicles to deploy very large philanthropy on behalf of donors. These also need to be for-profit venture philanthropy organizations that can charge a management fee to attract the teams with the skills in scaling companies, which are necessary to execute these deployments. They are providing an extremely sophisticated and valuable service and thus can be compensated with a market rate. These firms thus don't need to be a nonprofit to have gifts cover operational losses. Omidyar Networks has been able to attract investment professionals who have the skills in making deals and conducting due diligence and growth plans, such as private equity professionals, to lead the deployments of their philanthropic investments. These individuals have the experience in the rigorous investment process that makes successful private equity investments. Not having this experience in the team of large venture philanthropy organizations can put donor philanthropy at unnecessary risk. These individuals also need to have the knowledge and sensitivity of nonprofit cultures to navigate in a world with little planning and limited investments in management, despite their management teams being incredibly committed to their mission and their roles.

There is little surprise that Blue Meridian Partners is leading the way in large venture philanthropy deployments with a rigorous process similar to that of private equity. Chuck Harris, who has led much of the creation of

Blue Meridian Partners, has been dedicated since 2002 to increasing the amounts given by billionaires. He retired from Goldman Sachs as a partner in investment banking and therefore has an intimate knowledge of private equity and venture capital.

When I started my first job in private equity, I was taught that private equity is an apprenticeship business requiring many years of experience and mistakes to successfully deliver high investment returns. I saw many groups open and close offices in Latin America when I was there with Advent International. Experience is very important. Large venture philanthropy requires very similar skills needed to grow organizations successfully, making sure donor gifts are maximized and risks greatly reduced. But to do so requires professionals with those specific skills like Chuck.

As Dan Pallota explains in his 2013 Ted Talk,[14] if you are a nonprofit, you are expected to operate on a shoestring budget. Venture philanthropy at scale is not the solution to all problems but it is a path to greatly scale organizations effectively, especially as they look to break out of the Overhead Myth and invest in the areas required to grow and manage growth successfully. Growth can be very detrimental to an organization, especially one already run with limited management resources. Growth can bring pressure to systems, financial health, staff and management. There is a long history of private and publicly traded companies that failed when not ready for the stress of high growth.

In an attempt to fund our first Big Bets, I came across a way to deploy larger gifts with for-profits ready to quickly take them in to unlock great impact in their core businesses. With for-profit partners, we have designed our first vehicles to allow donors to outsource their large philanthropy to dedicated teams with private equity experience, who also have deep insight into nonprofit management. These two worlds need to be bridged so we can focus on highly replicable deals where philanthropy can unlock large-scale impact in housing, water infrastructure, climate change and others through later stage companies.

In our water deals, we will co-invest philanthropy along with private equity funds, and their water utilities, who are purchasing and upgrading distressed utilities that are currently not able to provide clean drinking water. As we drive more capital into this strategy, it could take $100 billion in philanthropy, we are creating a path to upgrade America's water infrastructure in a very targeted way and with very large measurable impact. The philanthropy will allow the private water utility to invest and upgrade these distressed utilities bringing clean water to more of the 21 million Americans who have polluted water in their homes. These areas have utilities that are truly abandoned and represent some of the most actionable and replicable investments in social justice and equity.

One of the benefits for philanthropists using their gifts in private situations is that they can benefit from for-profit management teams that are built for scale. U.S. water infrastructure is a good example. Private companies are rolling-up many of the 52,000 private water utilities in the U.S. We can prioritize the 5,000 ones generating polluted water to homes and upgrade them in areas to deliver clean water to their residents. These private companies and their investors are currently passing on acquisitions in poor U.S. communities with polluted water because the cost to fix the utilities is too high for their numbers to work. Philanthropy can unlock this impact by paying for enough of the costs for the investors to meet their returns, thus creating a win-win situation for all parties. Philanthropy makes the impact economical in their core business.

In a similar way, our affordable housing strategy blends philanthropy into affordable housing projects that leading national developers are brining online. This philanthropy unlocks great impact by allowing developers to replace debt, save interest expense and thus reduce rents permanently. They can set aside 300% more apartments for vulnerable populations, such as the homeless. These one-time philanthropic investments, which are highly replicable (1,000 of these buildings are started every year), generate permanent high impact. With philanthropy a great alchemy takes place where the developer can make their required return, each community has more deeply affordable apartments, more vulnerable populations are housed, and donors have clear, quantifiable and fulfilling impact.

I will also guess that MacKenzie Scott, and other innovative mega-philanthropists really looking to make a difference are experiencing this fulfilling impact, a joy that is defining who they are. It is a joy I see that is already a part of the DNA of the millennials and Gen-Ys at Columbia University and MIT that I have been working with in our projects. The push to impact will accelerate as it triggers this joy in those wholeheartedly pursing it. It takes grit to focus on creating a path into the unknown by the donors and the students. It's faith that failure is possible and likely, but it is getting easier to publicly take these risks as the impact is more visible with more scale.

Notes

1. South Florida Sun Sentinel, Lois K. Solomon, January 7, 2020, *Health care, shared housing focus of new plan to reduce homelessness*, https://www.sun-sentinel.com/local/palm-beach/fl-ne-pbc-plan-to-end-homelessness-20200107-unwvx5f4uvdstp7e5yzkgthhmy-story.html.

2. Business Insider, *The billionaire 'Giving Pledge' signed by Bill Gates and Elon Musk could soon be worth up to $600 billion*, Peter Kotecki, July 18, 2018, https://www.businessinsider.com/bill-gates-elon-musk-giving-pledge-may-reach-600-billion-2018-7.

3. Wealth-X Billionaire Census 2020, Wealth-X, https://www.wealthx.com/report/the-wealth-x-billionaire-census-2020/.

4. Gates Foundation gives millions to help persuade ultra-wealthy donors to give more of their billions, Mark Harris, GeekWire, January 23, 2021.

5. The Giving Pledge turns 10: These billionaires pledged to give away half their wealth, but they soon ran into a problem, MarketWatch, Leslie Albrecht, August 10, 2020, https://www.marketwatch.com/story/giving-away-money-well-is-very-hard-the-giving-pledge-turns-10-and-its-signers-are-richer-than-ever-2020-08-08.

6. Exclusive: The Billionaire Who Wanted To Die Broke... Is Now Officially Broke, Forbes, Steven Bertoni, September 15, 2020, https://www.forbes.com/sites/stevenbertoni/2020/09/15/exclusive-the-billionaire-who-wanted-to-die-brokeis-now-officially-broke/?sh=2bca6e8b3a2a.

7. Dr. James Finley, former Cistercian monk, student of Thomas Merton and clinical psychologist, Florida Atlantic University, Peaceful Life Series, Boca Raton, November 16, 2017.

8. MacKenzie Scott Has Donated More Than $4 Billion In Last 4 Months, NPR, Laurel Wamsley, December 16, 2020, https://www.npr.org/2020/12/16/947189767/mackenzie-scott-has-donated-more-than-4-billion-in-last-4-months.

9. Pledge Aside, Dead Billionaires Don't Have to Give Away Half Their Fortune, Bloomberg, Brendan Coffey June 4, 2015, https://www.bloomberg.com/news/articles/2015-06-04/as-billionaires-bask-in-glow-of-pledge-giving-half-is-optional.

10. The 2020 DAF Report, National Philanthropic Trust, https://www.nptrust.org/reports/daf-report/#:~:text=Contributions%20to%20DAFs%20in%202019,2019%2C%20which%20was%209.5%20percent.

11. Solving The Giving Pledge Bottleneck, Journal of Wealth Management, Paul G. Schervish, Sean A. Davis, Richard L. Cosnotti and Kirby S. Rosplock, Summer 2016, https://jwm.pm-research.com/content/19/1/23.

12. Company websites: New Profit https://www.newprofit.org/, Venture Philanthropy Partners http://www.vppartners.org/REDF https://redf.org.

13. Company website: REDF. https://redf.org/about/our-story/.

14. The Way We Think About Charity is Dead Wrong, Dan Pallota, Ted Talk, 2013, https://www.ted.com/talks/dan_pallotta_the_way_we_think_about_charity_is_dead_wrong?language=en.

"when you are traveling in...the stratosphere, although you may be going seven times as fast, you lose all sense of speed."
—Thomas Merton

6

Blockage

"How much do we leave our kids?"

In parallel to the impact on capitalism of The Giving Pledge and the ESG movement in asset management and on the corporate world globally, there is a third trend that is accelerating the potential financing of more good. It will also be creating more of a blockage in The Giving Pledge Bottleneck. Many high-profile philanthropists have been struggling to determine how much of their wealth they should leave their children. They are concerned with the negative impact large inheritances may have on their children's motivations to be productive and have meaningful careers and work lives. They have a sincere interest in promoting their children's well-being and understand how too large of an inheritance may be detrimental to this.

As more of the very wealthy consider this issue, it will also drive the availability of larger philanthropy. In addition, it will drive the need to have vehicles and managers to actively deploy these funds with high impact. Not only is the wealth of the richest individuals globally growing, more are reaching the category of being billionaires. In 2016, Forbes listed 1,826 billionaires with $7 trillion in assets. In 2020, it counted 2,096 after the downturn,[1] but Wealth-X reported 2,825 in its "The Billionaire Census" in the summer of 2020, a 8.5% increase from 2019.[2]

The good news is that there will continue to be philanthropic funds available to solve the world's most pressing social and environmental issues as these three trends increase. Yet the question persists: how do we attract and channel those funds? Do the ultra-wealthy not want to give? Can we give in to the cynicism? Is it just a lack of options? Is it a lack of marketing of the existing ones? Is it that the 2,825 billionaires aren't aware they can outsource their large philanthropy and enjoy more fulfilment? Is it the risk of large deployments into nonprofits without the strength of planning that for-profits have?

Beyond these billionaires, there are 150,000 individuals with $100 million or more, according to Wealth-X.[2] Therefore, it is important for us to encourage them too to give more of their funds while they are still alive. How do we reach them to let them know that large venture philanthropy organizations are here to help? It's not just as a matter of increasing giving, but for them to be able to enjoy the impact that their funds can generate.

Then, there is the question of "how much is enough?" A way to look at this question is to look at someone's annual spending. We can ask how much needs to be in a bank account at a wealth management firm to support that amount for the remainder of their lives and that of their children. Assuming an annual return after taxes of 5%, a family that has a total annual spending of $2 million would need just $40 million in this account forever. And that is if they are generating no other income from their business activities. This would cover all of the expenses associated with their homes, planes, boats, travel, education, philanthropy and other expenses. This assumes they also already have most of the homes, planes, boats and other expensive items they will purchase and that they don't need to make significant investments in their businesses or in starting new ones.

There is a point at which having more than $40 million for that family or individual may never be spent. Finding this point is a personal choice, but let's assume that having 3 times what is needed forever would be enough to feel secure. Or even 5 times that. At $200 million, the annual interest and gains would be $10 million after taxes.

If that individual or family has $500 million in assets, then I would argue that every dollar of the $300 million above the first $200 million has a marginal value of zero because it will almost surely never be used. Instead, $300 million could be used today for large impact philanthropy, in addition to the $8 million a year generated beyond the $2 million in annual spending. If that family has leading nonprofits or large venture philanthropy firms offering ways to deploy those funds to solve large challenges, and ways to also engage the family in doing so, then those dollars will go from having a marginal value of zero to having a very high value. Their value could be much higher than their face value, if this is done right. It too requires specialized talent that can manage sophisticated people in concierge-type services to allow donors and their families to experience the impact and the good their excess funds are making possible.

When the first housing development that I worked on opened, it was very fulfilling. It had been almost 2 years of work from start to finish. It was the first housing for single homeless women in the Palm Beach County. A major donor to our nonprofit, The Lord's Place, found out that we wanted to take the first step in correcting this awful reality. At the time, there were zero beds for homeless women if they were not with a family and could then qualify for family housing. There was housing for single men but not for single women, aside from a few beds available for victims of domestic violence. Our donor simply asked "how much?" We had no idea. We had not thought about any aspect of this except that we wanted to do it. His unanswered question was the starting point for us to develop our strategy, our focus, find the property, manage the remodelling of the property we bought, raise the funds and open its doors.

This same donor made introductions to the architects we used and stayed involved. Before the formal opening, he was able to meet the first women that moved in and heard their stories. They told horrific stories of abandonment, domestic violence, sexual abuse, drug and alcohol abuse, living in their cars, human trafficking and committing misdemeanours to be incarcerated to not go hungry or without shelter. They now had a beautiful home, opportunities to reinvent themselves and find self-sufficiency. They had hope and joy. Our donor experienced all this. The day of the ribbon cutting ceremony he could not make it through his speech without long pauses. He was crying as he was so moved that his gift and his involvement were resulting in these 10 women (and countless since) getting off the streets and the cars they were living in and into this beautiful residence named after him. It was very moving to see this strong gentleman, a successful businessman, moved to tears and just radiate with gratitude. His level of fulfilment was visible, even tangible and extraordinary.

A couple of days later, he called me to let me know that he was sending us another gift as large as the naming gift he made for the residence. I asked him what he wanted us to use the funds for. He said he knew that we didn't have a project but that his involvement was one of the most important experiences of his life. Not his gift, but his involvement. This is what we want to experience as philanthropists. Not just large gifts but being engaged in the project in order to maximize fulfilment. Every donor is different but I have found engagement is key and it is the gift we can give donors. To see change, to feel it and to reach that high level of fulfilment. Creating ways to have families experience this kind of fulfilment with much larger gifts is a challenge for a nonprofit that is already spread thin for resources. Larger venture philanthropy firms can take the lead here. They can attract specialized executives to engage these donors and their families to witness the impact beyond the traditional gift-making.

As an ecosystem of nonprofit managers, philanthropists, wealth advisors, estate attorneys, venture philanthropists, foundations, philanthropy advisors, governments and others, we need to encourage the creation of more venture philanthropy firms to create larger giving opportunities and to engage philanthropists to increase their fulfilment. The private equity skillsets of supporting and growing organizations, as well as those from other industries, are critical to create the plans, structure and deploy the funds, and most importantly, actively support the management teams creating impact on a regular basis. But helping philanthropists experience the impact and have fulfilment is where the heart is moved. In the process, those dollars that have low marginal value become dollars with incredible value.

Everyone gains when we are mindful about how much is enough and about giving the rest away for the good of all, including the donors, their families and their children. It is key to increase the well-being of children of those who can give more in order to not sap their motivation to work and diligently apply themselves to their careers or vocations. It can also be an incredible long-term opportunity to increase it by generating fulfilment through very well-managed, detailed strategies of giving away large funds and engaging them in the process. These decisions will drive how much more capital will be available to fund change at scale.

Our donor took the time to slow down and involve himself in our new residential program. UHNWI can lead very busy lives, and they can miss this type of experience and this life-changing opportunity. We have to invite them to slow down by presenting and engaging them long term in solutions that are visible and have measurable impact at scale.

Notes

1. Dolan, K.A., and L. Kroll. "Inside the 2015 Forbes Billionaires List: Facts and Figures." Forbes.com, March 2, 2015, http://www.forbescom/sites/kerryadolan/2015/03/02/inside-the-2015-forbes-billionaires-list-facts-and-figures/#2b9e839a6cec.

2. Wealth-X Billionaire Census 2020, Wealth-X, https://www.wealthx.com/report/the-wealth-x-billionaire-census-2020/.

"Solitude is not something you must hope for in the future. Rather, it is a deepening of the present, and unless you look for it in the present you will never find it."
—Thomas Merton

7

Buried by Wealth

The signers of The Giving Pledge are some of the most successful entrepreneurs and financiers of all time. As many continue to own their companies or a part of them, and we continue to benefit from a rising stock market, much of their wealth continues to grow at impressive rates. At the same time, giving rates continue to be limited.

The Giving Pledge Bottleneck is therefore growing and even those who are the most generous are not able to keep their giving ahead of their annual returns, with many of them falling drastically behind. According to Chuck Collins, since 2010, the wealth of the original 62 signers of The Giving Pledge has almost doubled. These are the ones who are still alive, and their wealth has grown from $376 billion to $734 billion.[1] If giving away half of $376 billion is not daunting enough, giving away half of $734 billion is even more daunting.

Just from March to July 2020, the wealth of the 100 U.S. signers increased 28% or $214 billion in 4 months.[1] How can they keep their pledges with such dramatic increase in wealth? Chuck Collins also states that there is also $1.2 trillion in private foundations and over $140 billion in ungifted DAFs[2] that needs a home as well.

As mentioned previously, there was a great bright spot in giving in 2020. The $1.7 billion in gifts from MacKenzie Scott has been a great step forward to encourage more philanthropists to give faster and in larger amounts. A few

© The Author(s), under exclusive license to Springer Nature
Switzerland AG 2021
S. Davis, *Solving the Giving Pledge Bottleneck*,
https://doi.org/10.1007/978-3-030-78865-0_7

months later, she shocked the world of philanthropy with an additional $4.7 billion in gifts. She continues to give record amounts and has been greatly praised for only giving large unrestricted gifts, a great departure from the restricted nature of very large philanthropy. Although this is also an example of great giving, it may still be falling greatly behind the gains on her portfolio in the previous 18 months. Let alone as a small percentage of her wealth before that time. How do you give half away when your giving can't keep up with increases in wealth?

It is important to reiterate what was reported in 2015 in Bloomberg.com that 10 Giving Pledge signers had passed since signing the pledge and that they did not seemingly give half their wealth to nonprofits, especially beyond any family foundation. If the goal is to experience the fulfilment of giving in life, we can assume the goal is to give it away faster, before we lose out of time.

Given average life spans, we are heading into more examples of unfunded pledges. According to the Center for Disease Control and Prevention, the average lifespan in the U.S. was 78.6 years in a 2017 study.[3] And according to Elena McCollim and Hans Peter Schmitz from the University of San Diego, the average age of The Giving Pledge signers was 70 years old in 2019.[4] This would suggest that as a whole about $600 billion needs to be giving away in less than 10 years. This is a 2022 estimate of the value of The Giving Pledge benefits, but does not account for asset growth over the next decade.[5] A more realistic number may be $1.2 trillion, as it also assumes there are no new signers, and it's important for many more to sign The Giving Pledge.

If we were to look at average asset growth and assume certain giving rates for all of The Giving Pledge signers, we can see the magnitude of the giving that is required. The $600 billion that needs to be given away could quickly grow into $1.2 trillion or more within 10 years at a 10% growth rate. And given average age spans, we could conclude that gifts would have to be made at much higher rates than current average signer giving rates. A flat 25% giving rate over 10 years would be one way to achieve the goal of having the singers meet their pledges. But this would start with $150 billion in gifts in 2021.

A ramp-up in giving would also achieve the goal starting with a 10% gift rate on the $600 billion and growing to a 50% rate in year 10. But that is still a large hurdle at $60 billion in new gifts at first. A large check today can always be made to fulfill a pledge. Any nonprofit anywhere could accept a large gift to endow funds to help permanently cover part of its operating costs. But I believe signers of The Giving Pledge are sincerely interested in changing the world. They are interested in funding solutions. They want to give their funds to something that is well managed, that makes a difference but also visibly moves the needle on solving an issue. These opportunities are not readily available at scale.

Across the U.S., there are thousands of capital campaigns taking place on any given day. According to the Chronicle of Philanthropy, about 46% of nonprofits were in either a capital or a special campaign during the first half of 2016, up from a mere 12% in 2011, and another 28% said they were planning a campaign.[6] So there is no shortage of giving opportunities, although almost all have dispersed impact. It is a school classroom here, a church parish hall addition there, a hospital robotic surgery machine, or a new homeless residential unit or an extension of your local animal rescue organization. These are all critical and important activities, many addressing great unmet needs. They are also not part of a detailed solution for the entire problem.

A lack of giving opportunities at scale to fund solutions is also driving The Giving Pledge Bottleneck. Can this be avoided? In one word, yes. We have many examples we can look at where other forms of capital were organized to be deployed in larger amounts over time. The capital was institutionalized. Many asset classes were just cottage industries a couple of decades ago and they were not a large part of the financial system. Venture capital and private equity are good examples.

Even these were frontier sectors of finance once. Groups of early adopters sought to deploy more funds in private situations. These were not publicly traded investments, with any liquidity for investors. They were the opposite. They were investments in private companies that would take many years to realize any gains from. In the meantime, these early investors had to work with the management teams of the companies they backed to create value in terms of growth, increasing profitability, using leverage or creating attractive exit opportunities.

Venture capital and private equity investments have slowly become more widely understood and admired for their ability to deliver returns in ways that were not correlated to public markets. These investments were very active as they required the managers of these funds to be present in the companies, sit on their boards and bring "more than just money" to the table. They had to actively add value. This became very interesting to institutional investors who committed larger funds to these early managers. As more managers emerged, the allocations continued to increase and today these direct investments are a key part of finance globally.

After spending a few years building large growth plans for nonprofits, I realized there are limitations to funding larger amounts given how much we have starved them for resources and penalized them from making investments in management, fundraising, planning and management systems.

I came across the idea using for-profits as more efficient vehicles to deploy mega-philanthropy. These include blending philanthropy in buyouts and real estate development to unlock great impact. This is something the IRS allows as long as there is a "good" being achieved, as seen for decades in the use of Program Related Investments (PRI) by foundations. We can use a direct investing approach to find, structure, oversee and report on the impact.

Large philanthropists could then commit large gifts every year to philanthropy funds making these deployments and outsource the process, much like they outsource their venture capital and private equity returns to firms actively making those investments. As more and more groups offer these alternatives, Giving Pledge signers can allocate larger and larger amounts of their annual philanthropy to them. Venture philanthropy at scale can help take in these larger funds.

Notes

1. In a pandemic, billionaires are richer than ever. Why aren't they giving more?, Chuck Collins, August 3, 2020, *The Guardian.*
2. The 2020 DAF Report, National Philanthropic Trust, https://www.nptrust.org/reports/daf-report/#:~:text=Contributions%20to%20DAFs%20in%202019,2019%2C%20which%20was%209.5%20percent.
3. Center for Disease Control and Prevention, National Vital Statistics Reports, United States Life Tables 2017, June 24, 2019, Elizabeth Arias, Ph.D., and Jiaquan Xu, M.D.
4. A Golden Age of Philanthropy? An Analysis of The Giving Pledge's Commitment Letters, Paper presented at the Symposium Philanthropy & Social Impact, The Center of Philanthropy & Public, March 14–16, 2019, Elena McCollim, Hans Peter Schmitz.
5. A billionaire who signed The Giving Pledge in 2012 said Bill Gates' philanthropy pact isn't 'growing as rapidly as we hoped,' Business Insider, Taylor Nicole Rogers, October 24, 2019, https://www.businessinsider.com/billionaire-signed-giving-pledge-isnt-growing-rapidly-as-hoped-2019-10#:~:text=The%20Giving%20Pledge%20could%20be%20worth%20%24600%20billion%20by%202022&text=The%20pledge%20now%20has%20204,research%20firm%20Wealth%2DX%20found.

6. Capital Campaigns Increasingly Common, and They Work, Study Says, Heather Joslyn, January 4, 2016, The Chronicle of Philanthropy.

"...if we don't understand the end we will make a wrong use of the means."
—Thomas Merton

8

How We Got Here

It is easy to look at The Giving Pledge and conclude that it is an attempt to take credit on a global stage with little accountability and that signers have no interest in actually doing anything beyond taking credit. Yet it is important to note that The Giving Pledge has already been a great success from an advocacy point of view.

Is there anyone who is hugely successful who has not heard of The Giving Pledge? Has it not become a new measuring stick for success? And if so, has it permanently changed the goalposts of capitalism? I would guess that every uber-successful individual in the world is asking themselves what good can they do. If some of the wealthiest and admired investors and entrepreneurs on the planet have signalled their intent to give half their fortune away to generate impact, how does this affect all those following behind? They may be asking themselves "what impact am I going to have on the world?"

Clearly, The Giving Pledge is not occurring on its own but is part of a larger rising tide of good in the world. It is very complimentary to the ESG movement and to other changes in capitalism such as the Business Roundtable announcement in 2019[1] rejecting that corporations only focus on shareholder value. So, in the sense of inspiring others to commit to give more in life, The Giving Pledge is a great success. It has become an advocacy movement to prioritize larger giving today.

© The Author(s), under exclusive license to Springer Nature
Switzerland AG 2021
S. Davis, *Solving the Giving Pledge Bottleneck*,
https://doi.org/10.1007/978-3-030-78865-0_8

The next questions are more complex and result from the inherent innovation in this movement. What happens when someone agrees to give away $500 million or more? What if they have never done that before? And what if there is no institutional way to deploy those funds. Unlike other forms of capital where there are investment bankers, private placement agents, venture capital and private equity managers to rapidly deploy funds, philanthropy, aside from a handful of exceptions, does not have these.

Foundations at least have professional staff who help chart the course of the giving of a foundation. Their jobs include giving away at least 5% of the funds of the foundation annually, so that they can maintain their 501(c)(3) status while doing the good they exist to do. They also have to look at the areas of need they want to focus on, build the relationships with the management teams of the nonprofits in their areas, evaluate proposals, fund them, report on impact to their boards and look for ways to be innovative by collaborating with other funders.

There is also an ecosystem of advisors who can help foundations and philanthropists strategize about areas of interest and ways to optimize their giving. There is very little help though in terms of advisors to whom they can outsource the entire philanthropic process at scale. Advisors who interface with the nonprofits and help the management teams of the nonprofits chart a course for higher growth and higher impact. This more "active" advisory work borrows from the venture capital and private equity direct investing approach which is considered more active as they are inside the companies, sitting on the boards, creating strategy and overseeing growth over the long term.

These active advisors are the venture philanthropy firms that exist at a "venture" level today and are beginning to arise at the larger levels. Without these players and without the equivalent of investment bankers and private placement agents, there are only limited ways that philanthropists can gift into nonprofits. More importantly, the nonprofits do not have the ability to take in large dollar amounts, resulting in The Giving Pledge Bottleneck.

With this in mind, how can the signers of The Giving Pledge adequately fulfill their commitments if the nonprofits that can take in these funds are not presenting them with opportunities to take in $100 million every week. Are we to expect philanthropists to quit their day jobs to dedicate themselves full-time to give away their funds? Of course, they could give all of their gifts to any nonprofit and let them spend the funds or they could endow their operations forever. Any nonprofit would gladly take their funds.

As most of us would agree, the question of giving away a fortune is not to be taken lightly. What happens if the funds are not well deployed? What happens if little impact results? This criticism has often been levied against Mark Zuckerberg's $100 million gift as part of the $200 million initiative for the Newark School system.[2] Progress was made and the funds resulted in a good being generated, yet it was not the expected result of a revolutionary gift that was going to be a game-changer in education.

Even at a much smaller level donors worry significantly about the nonprofit's ability to be a good steward of a major gift. Making a gift of a much higher magnitude compounds these concerns. It is widely accepted that nonprofits try to use their limited funds as efficiently as possible. As an industry, the nonprofit world has inherent limitations that drive The Giving Pledge Bottleneck.

The overhead ratio has been a useful tool to look at nonprofits in a standard way, yet it has had drastic consequences. As Dan Pallota has successfully argued, a focus on overhead causes us to look at cost controls rather than increases in impact and growth. Traditionally, if a nonprofit spends less than 20% on overhead (management and fundraising), it is a "great" nonprofit. If it spends more, it is a "terrible" one.[3] But there is no looking at how much good it is doing, how many more people it is helping or what the overall impact is.

Because of the emphasis on the overhead ratio, there is a chronic underinvestment in management, management training and other critical components of growing a nonprofit. As a result, nonprofits are not generally growing, and they are not set up to receive a $200 million gift to engage in significant growth. Growth can be a terrible thing for an organization that lacks management with extensive experience in high growth situations, as discussed earlier.

Another result of the emphasis on the overhead ratio is that nonprofits always have to limit the amount of financial compensation they can offer (hence the quality of the talent it can attract). Much of the management of nonprofits are very dedicated but poorly compensated and many need an additional job to be able to cover their expenses. To expect these individuals to quickly transition into a high growth environment with no long-term training is not possible, and already, many managers of nonprofits have two or three full-time roles within the organization. The philosophy is often "I know you need $3 to run your own department but we are going to give you $1 and so do the best you can."

A key area where this approach creates a serious issue is in the area of planning. Most nonprofits do not have the luxury to have staff that are proficient in planning, and thus, there are very few large-scale, detailed long-term plans. Most managing in a nonprofit is done focusing on a one-year budget. Much grant making is not multi-year, which makes this challenge even greater. Where there is a long-term view, it is mostly within the context of a capital campaign. Capital campaigns are very specific in terms of costs and the funds are for specific uses, mostly one-time expenses like a new building, a new piece of hospital equipment, and not part of an attempt to greatly scale an organization.

What has resulted is a Catch 22 where there are large funders who have a desire to give more but lack large giving opportunities that move the needle on an issue. Every community has a capital campaign for a new school, church addition or hospital expansion. Yet almost no giving opportunities exist to solve any major social or environmental challenge in any community. Planning and focusing on modelling solutions is a path to do that. "But if nonprofit management team members are already doing three jobs, it is unrealistic to expect them to develop detailed and compelling long-term plans to scale their organization and actually solve the problem they have set out to conquer."

Solutions do exist. The funds are there. Yet they are not coming together. Most nonprofits are fighting to keep the lights on and the work they are doing is critical and very important. We have to complement this work with more and larger vehicles to bridge the gap between where they are and what the solutions are.

Notes

1. Business Roundtable Redefines the Purpose of a Corporation to Promote 'An Economy That Serves All Americans', August 19, 2019, Business Roundtable, https://www.businessroundtable.org/business-roundtable-redefines-the-purpose-of-a-corporation-to-promote-an-economy-that-serves-all-americans.
2. Mark Zuckerberg once made a $100 million investment in a major US city to help fix its schools—now the mayor says the effort 'parachuted' in and failed, Leanna Garfield, May 12, 2018, https://www.businessinsider.com/mark-zucker berg-schools-education-newark-mayor-ras-baraka-cory-booker-2018-5.

3. The Way We Think About Charity is Dead Wrong, Dan Pallota, Ted Talk, 2013, https://www.ted.com/talks/dan_pallotta_the_way_we_think_about_charity_is_dead_wrong?language=en.

"The secret of interior peace is detachment."
—Thomas Merton

9

Venture Philanthropy at the Venture Level

The structural challenges of the nonprofit world are not new. There is also a long history of improvements through the work of venture philanthropy organizations going back 20 years. The natural conclusion of these structural challenges is the need for long-term plans, investments in management, improved systems and well-funded initiatives over several years. The venture philanthropy industry has been doing this while applying venture capital approaches to the nonprofit world.

The term and the concept of venture philanthropy were first published in a Harvard Business Review article in April 1997.[1] It argued that foundations could apply a rigorous venture capital process into their giving. Venture capitalists engage in very detailed due diligence, risk evaluation and mitigation, performance measurement, modelling of growth of revenue, profitability and cash flow, as well as exit and return assumptions. This is all before the investment. And this is only the beginning as suggested by the venture capital and private equity adage: "the work starts after the investment."

Venture philanthropy cannot solve all issues. It can be used to scale specific nonprofits and support specific management teams and equip them with many of the resources they need today. Many solutions are local and often global challenges require system-based solutions. In other words, nonprofits need to work together with other stakeholders to solve a challenge as having one huge nonprofit doing one thing well may not solve the whole challenge. Poverty in the U.S. is a good example. Place-based initiatives like the Harlem Children Zone and Purpose Built Communities are early examples at success in eliminating poverty in a very specific area, with a systems-based multi-party approach.

In 2016, I discovered that bleak neighborhoods could be turned around. I never knew something like this was possible. East Lake, in Atlanta, was

© The Author(s), under exclusive license to Springer Nature Switzerland AG 2021
S. Davis, *Solving the Giving Pledge Bottleneck*,
https://doi.org/10.1007/978-3-030-78865-0_9

a bleak neighborhood with tremendous challenges that Tom Cousins was able to turn around. He had been inspired by a New York Times Article that said that 70% of New York State prison inmates come from just six neighborhoods in New York City.[2] He thus set out to turn around bleak neighborhoods. Today, we now know that where you are born is key to your success, and being born in a distressed neighborhood results in significant toxic trauma. This impedes healthy neurological and physiological development and with many other hurdles, drives inter-generational urban poverty in America.

Tom Cousins led a group of community leaders, philanthropists, educators, real estate developers and wellness specialists to invest in a very defined neighborhood (East Lake) to create meaningful change. Over a 10-year period, they completed life-changing investments in affordable housing (for-profit), education (K-12 "cradle to college" education covering early learning, a leading charter school and after-school programs such as the First-Tee golf program), wellness (a beautiful glass YMCA community center) and many others assets.

At every level, the children and residents of East Lake experienced impressive improvements and the neighborhood health became an example of success for others to follow. After visiting East Lake, Warren Buffet and Julian Robertson decided to create a nonprofit with Tom Cousins to take this success to other cities. Purpose Built Communities was created to replicate the East Lake success. Since then, Purpose Built Communities has initiated over 27 turnarounds across the country acting as a value-added consultant to cities that want to replicate their model with key local differences.[3] One of the trademarks of Purpose Built is that they spend two years visiting with local neighborhood leaders, local philanthropists, developers, government officials and others to foster local buy-in and establish locally led leadership for the initiative. Each turn-around project borrows lessons from each other and is separately led and funded.

At the time, I met with Purpose Built's CEO David Edwards as they were invited by the City of West Palm Beach, to help them start a turnaround of one of their challenging neighborhoods. When David was visiting, he met with my students and me at Palm Beach Atlantic University. They were so excited with David and the Purpose Built Communities approach that they decided to write a business plan for the local Purpose Built initiative as their class project. David asked me what I did. At the time, I was in my first year of looking to create vehicles to deploy the Giving Pledge-type funds that were stuck and not moving into solutions. So it was hard to explain that I had started a firm that was doing venture philanthropy work but at a larger level and I was looking to scale nonprofits with $100 million or more. Instead, I asked what I've asked many nonprofit CEOs: "if you could bring you all the money in the world, what would you do?"

David thought about it and said that there are 825 neighborhoods that are the most abandoned bleak neighborhoods in America where the 10 million most inter-generational urban poor live. He would turn those around. I follow-up with, "So how much?" This is clearly the type of rhetorical question that we need to be asking for every single social and environmental challenge we have. They are straightforward simple questions which require much focused work to answer well. But it's no more complex work than creating the detailed projections of publicly traded international companies with diversified holdings. We need to be able to attract and pay for those with the skills to do this kind of planning if we want to solve our challenges.

This is the key inflection point we are in. The Giving Pledge signers have changed the way we look at solutions because for the first time ever we can actually fund the solutions. We can use philanthropy to bring the skilled talent missing to upgrade struggling systems to get ready to scale, to invest in operations and expansion, to develop performance contracts and Social Impact Bonds funded with philanthropy that can bring long-term sustainability at a higher level, and all of this because the funds are there. More importantly, there is also now more of a general solutions-based perspective. The signers know first-hand that you get what you pay for, and that if you want to solve a problem you need to bring the skills and funds missing to execute the solutions. Because of all this, I believe we are in the most significant inflection point in the history of philanthropy.

Scaling nonprofit solutions that exist, scaling systems that complement each other, getting local buy-in and leadership, and the funds to do so are now possible. Many of the solutions will start with large philanthropy and be followed up with larger government grants once the solutions are proven and cost savings are delivered to communities. One of the main benefits of Social Impact Bonds and more scalable performance contracts is they are designed to show and prove effective ways for government funds to be spent in a way that solves problems. All the elements contributing to this rising tide of good will also make it easier for governments to more actively pursue solutions that yield real cost savings and healthier communities.

Venture philanthropy is a key piece of this transformation as it starts with creating comprehensive detailed multi-year plans. The planning, modelling and project management skills and systems are readily available in the for-profit world. Yet they cannot be applied to nonprofit solutions within the current overhead ratio mindset of the nonprofit world. I have been a part of many meetings in the homeless services space where these types of investments were shied away from because leadership knew how negatively donors could react if our overhead ratio rose above 20%, even if we were investing in management and systems that would actually help us raise more money and spend it more efficiently in fulfilling our mission. This is all changing, and it starts with planning and developing credible, well-developed answers to the question "How much?"

As David Gladstone wrote in The Venture Capital Handbook,[4] venture capitalists are focused "adding more than just money" for companies. This "active" management of funds is based around creating value in the companies funded by assisting the entrepreneurs with new clients, hiring senior managers with strong track records, upgrading company systems, creating long-term plans providing this kind of value-added assistance over the long term. As sales grow and profitability increases, venture capitalists help create the value that their compensation is based on. Traditionally venture capital investors receive a 2% management fee and 20% of the profits on their investments. This is usually after them refunding their management fee and after an 8% hurdle rate for investors.

Starting over 20 years ago, several cutting-edge nonprofit organizations created the U.S. venture philanthropy industry. New Profit, REDF, Venture Philanthropy Partners and several others started receiving gifts on behalf of philanthropists and engaging in the active management of these funds. They played a role in increasing the growth as well as improving management training and systems of leading nonprofits. There are several foundations like The Robinhood Foundation that have also applied more rigorous ways of measuring and tracking the outputs and outcomes of the nonprofits they fund. Individuals, foundations and corporations in the U.S. jointly gave $449.6 billion in 2019.[5] As their giving adopts venture philanthropy methods, more impact will be generated nationally.[6]

Key aspects of venture philanthropy also include a long-term commitment to support an organization, a holistic view of the entire operation (rather than a particular program), and can include taking a board seat at the nonprofit. A centrepiece of the value-added work in venture philanthropy is helping nonprofits to identify, recruit and train excellent top management. This mirrors the private equity saying "What are the 3 most important things in successful private equity investing? Management, management and management."

Europe, Asia and Latin America also have a small yet active venture philanthropy industry. In almost all cases, the venture philanthropy work and the funding have been done at the "venture" level. The size of grants is usually less than $1 million. Most of the main players report publicly that their total grants have been between $80 and $325 million over 20 years. Although these grants have laid the groundwork to apply these techniques to the nonprofit world, these funds do not have the ability to create the next Amazon, unlike their for-profit venture capital counterparts.

Venture capital investments can yield great increases in the value of company shares, creating currency to hire top talent and to acquire other companies, some of which is generated by the quality of the venture capital firm investing in them. Their valuable equity gives them fuel for financing growth that nonprofits don't have as they build their operations towards generating cash flows to further grow. Nonprofits generally don't generate but require more cash to grow. Venture capital firms also help raise follow-up investments giving start-ups the runway to become greatly profitable and thus sustain themselves at very large scale.

Unfortunately, nonprofits can become less sustainable as they grow. As most of their income comes from philanthropic gifts, a larger scale means a need for a larger donor base. Yet growth is needed as there are so many social and environmental challenges globally. And many of these challenges cannot be addressed on a for-profit basis. Therefore, the organizations addressing these issues have to be nonprofits in order to offset losses from the work that they do. A clear example is a soup kitchen that is feeding the homeless cannot charge to feed its clients. The lack of income makes the costs to operate uneconomical without grants.

One very successful example of a nonprofit supported by venture philanthropy is KIPP, the Knowledge is Power Program network of charter schools preparing low-income children from early learning to college readiness. The founders started KIPP in 1994 and have now reached 255 schools and 100,000 students. Their 2016 990 reports total revenue of $139 million.[7] This is very impressive growth considering only 144 nonprofits of the 200,000 founded since 1970 that have crossed the $50 million in revenue level.[8] KIPP was an "investee partner" of New Profit from 2006 to 2014. During that period, KIPP grew from 45 schools to 200.

Notes

1. Harvard Business Review, April 1997, Virtuous Capital: What Foundations Can Learn from Venture Capitalists".
2. Tougher is Dumber, Todd Clear, The New York Times, December 4, 1993.
3. Poverty and Place, A Review of the Science and Research that has Impacted our Work, Purpose Built Communities, 2019, https://purposebuiltcommunities.org/wp-content/uploads/2020/06/Poverty-and-Place-White-Paper-Digital-Edition.pdf.
4. David Gladstone, The Venture Capital Handbook.
5. Giving USA 2020: The Annual Report on Philanthropy for the Year 2019, a publication of Giving USA Foundation, 2020, researched and written by the Indiana University Lilly Family School of Philanthropy. Available online at www.givingusa.org.
6. Websites: New Profit, www.newprofit.org, Venture Philanthropy Partners, www.vppartners.org, REDF, www.redf.org.
7. Knowledge is Power Project (KIPP), www.kipp.org.
8. How Nonprofits Get Really Big, Stanford University Innovation Review, William Foster and Gail Fine, Spring 2007.

"The only true joy on earth is to escape from the prison of our own false self."
—Thomas Merton

10

Venture Philanthropy at Scale

One of the most exciting developments in philanthropy and social impact has been the rise of venture philanthropy firms focused on making larger gifts for scale. The last 5 years have seen the emergence of players looking to deploy larger philanthropy into nonprofits on behalf of donors at previously unseen levels. This is similar to the spectrum of private equity investments which range from the small, early-stage venture capital level to larger growth equity and buyout levels.

These emerging larger venture philanthropy organizations are using different terms to describe what they are doing, yet they are all operating at a higher scale of giving than traditional venture philanthropy. These include "collaborative philanthropy" and "capital aggregation." I consider them large venture philanthropy firms as they exhibit similar venture philanthropy models and structures in their "active" attempts to support nonprofits in scaling in remarkable ways. They also follow the venture capital model of adding value beyond funding. The teams of these organizations are deeply involved in creating detailed growth plans, attracting specialized consultants, supporting management in thinking about hiring talent, upgrading systems and creating partnerships with other nonprofits and government entities, to not just get bigger but to solve systemic issues at the root of our social and environmental challenges. Many are deeply local issues with different histories, key players and dynamics that need to be incorporated if solutions are to be achieved.

It is difficult to make larger philanthropic gifts with higher impact, and it is a very hands-on work, which many large philanthropists have been

S. Davis, *Solving the Giving Pledge Bottleneck*, https://doi.org/10.1007/978-3-030-78865-0_10

outsourcing to these organizations. They are actively managing the funds committed to them in ways similar to how these same mega-donors outsource their venture capital investments in their family office portfolios to specialized venture capital firms. As discussed previously, the heart of venture philanthropy incorporates the key lesson of private equity: "What are the three most important things in private equity? Management, management, management." How can we identify, support and enhance the management teams of the nonprofits we want to scale, especially considering that they have traditionally been starved of resources for training and systems? Are they ready to scale? Given the historic scarcity, the answer is usually "no." This has contributed greatly to The Giving Pledge Bottleneck.

How do you deploy $200 million or $1 billion into an organization that has not grown at accelerated rates and has been penalized if their overhead ratio showed that they spend more than 20% on management and fundraising costs? Do we ignore all the for-profit businesses that have buckled under the pressure of high growth, or that pursued failed strategies simply because they had the capital to keep going down the wrong path? Running a high growth company is not a skill many managers in the for-profit world have. This is the case in the nonprofit world as well. This is why there is such an incredible lack of detailed 5- or 10-year growth plans in the nonprofit world. The good news is that these larger venture philanthropy organizations are leading the way to overcome these challenges.

Blue Meridian Partners stays truest to the private equity model on which venture philanthropy is based. Their donors are "General Partners" ($50 million minimum) or "Impact Partners" (previously called "Limited Partners"—$15 million minimum) that make philanthropic "commitments;" several of these are private equity terms. Blue Meridian, with the help of Bridgespan, also helps the nonprofits they back to build detailed 5 or 10-year plans showing what their $200 million in gifts would do over that time. As discussed, this type of detailed long-term plan is extremely rare in the nonprofit world. They have over $2 billion in commitments from prominent philanthropists and foundations.

Other organizations that are engaging in venture philanthropy work at the larger gift levels include Co-Impact, The Audacious Project and The End Fund. They have different levels of active management of the funds committed to them or the projects they sponsor for large philanthropists. They arose as more and more mega-philanthropists recognized the difficulty to get funds "out the door" and the difficulties they are experiencing to meet their Giving Pledge commitments. Just being able to give more money away to stay ahead of the annual growth of their assets in a growing economy and rising stock market would be a great improvement. This has proven almost impossible to do.

The established venture philanthropy firms, making smaller gifts, have also been third–party organizations providing an outsourcing service for philanthropists. They have also focused on making gifts and adding value beyond funds, and almost always multi-year giving. Given the size of their gifts, these firms have given in aggregate over $80 million each over 20 years. Some quite more than this. Yet one "Big Bet" from these new larger venture philanthropy organizations at $200 million is larger than some of their cumulative historic giving.

Besides funding larger-scale good by backing nonprofits to grow faster, larger venture philanthropy firms have started to provide the beginnings of an outlet for mega-philanthropists looking to give away large amounts effectively. They can outsource larger philanthropic funds to them. One of the main characteristics of these organizations is that several billionaires collaborate to pool their funds in order that these organizations lead the scaling of nonprofits that are ready to grow dramatically.

Blue Meridian Partners is making the largest Big Bets on the planet, and in the process, they are deploying funds on behalf of some of the best known and active philanthropists globally: Bill and Melinda Gates, Steve and Connie Ballmer, McKenzie Scott and Sergey Brin and about 14 other large funders. Blue Meridian was started in 2017 at the Edna McConnell Clark Foundation ("EMCF") in New York. EMCF was already pursuing scale for its nonprofits by funding fewer nonprofits with larger dollar amounts. Now spun-off, Blue Meridian is spending the remainder of EMCF's funds (about $1 billion) and has raised another $1 billion or so in commitments from these philanthropists. It is mainly scaling the 10 nonprofits it started to scale, each with about $200 million over 10 years.

Charles "Chuck" Harris joined EMCF to start this capital aggregation strategy as he has been trying to get billionaires to give larger gifts for about 15 years since leaving Goldman Sachs, where he held various investment banking leadership roles. Given his knowledge of private equity, Chuck created the path forward to institutionalize the deployment of large philanthropic gifts. Given that this is the largest pool of capital that is not actively managed, Chuck, along with the leadership of Blue Meridian, has quite literally changed philanthropy and finance in opening the door for this new sector of larger direct investing.

The direct investing of philanthropic funds will be a profitable area for financial institutions, advisors and newer firms outsourcing the giving of mega-philanthropists and becoming active managers, just like in other segments of direct investing. Arranging philanthropic capital raises, with roadshows in order to "place" funds into "philanthropic deals," will require fees to be paid to banks, private placement agencies and others for the work needed to make the funds be moved professionally. This further institutionalization will only benefit philanthropists and those suffering today, as more capital can move into solutions.

Co-Impact was also started in 2017 with a $500 million commitment from the Rockefeller Foundation and has a similarly strong roster of billionaire philanthropists allocating gifts to the nonprofits it supports: Jeff Skoll, Richard Chandler, Bill and Melinda Gates and MacKenzie Scott amongst many others. It seems to have less of an active management approach than Blue Meridian and is focused on scaling systems of change in the developing world. Their multi-year commitments are $10 to $50 million over a period of 5 years.

The Audacious Project is focused on curating large giving opportunities for its group of billionaire philanthropists, and it does not take in the funds nor does it manage them directly. Sponsored by TED, the organization famous for hosting Ted Talks, The Audacious Projects finds and promotes large giving opportunities to its donors, which include Richard Branson, Ray Dalio, Bill and Melinda Gates, Laura and John Arnold, Steve and Connie Ballmer, MacKenzie Scott and Jeff Skoll.

This is just the beginning. Many more steps need to be taken and many more players need to get involved to institutionalize this area of finance. Whether you consider large venture philanthropy to be a part of the nonprofit world, the world of foundations or asset management, the reality is that these early players can continue to plant the necessary seeds to build a strong delivery system of capital to scalable good. The human skills need to match the sophisticated work and the good news is that they are available in the investment banking, management consulting, venture capital and private equity worlds.

The function venture philanthropists provide is outsourcing. Outsourcing the hard work of pursuing scale to solve challenges can be given to these value-added service providers. It frees up philanthropists' focus, but more importantly, it brings specialized skills which are needed more and more if scaling is to be successful. Venture philanthropy at scale requires the specialized skills to help nonprofit CEOs grow their organizations at faster rates than they have ever done. This not only introduces hope for solutions to be attained but also introduces risks that are obvious and many that are unforeseen.

After decades of private equity success and failures at the heart of the global economy, there are thousands of specialized investment professionals, consultants, advisors and others that have cut their teeth succeeding—and more importantly failing—in growing companies. Seed investors like Tim Connors of PivotNorth Capital in Silicon Valley, early venture capital firms such as Benchmark, Kleiner Perkins, growth equity firms such as General Atlantic and later stage and restructuring private equity firms like KKR, Advent International, Texas Pacific Group, Bain Capital and many others have been making investments on behalf of investors to expand and improve companies.

These are higher risk investments than mutual funds and therefore require very specialized skills that are honed out of years of sitting on the boards of companies they have invested in over many years. It is called private equity as they are traditionally private companies that are illiquid. Unlike publicly-traded companies that mutual funds typically invest it, private equity investors are stuck until they find a way to exit their investments. Aside from a sale or IPO, there is not a readily available way to exit a private investment and in order for private equity managers to make a return for their investors and for themselves, they need to create value.

As mentioned earlier, the four main ways to create value in private equity are to grow the company, increase the profitability, use leverage and exit at higher multiples. Sometimes just one of these is enough to make the 10–20% annual returns these managers need to achieve to be able to raise another fund and stay in business. Ideally, all four can be used to create value and generate more cash for the investors. I remember looking for investments we could make in Latin America while I was with Advent International during our first fund starting in 1998. As an Associate in this global private equity firm, I was tasked with finding private companies we could invest in. Sometimes this was looking at companies we had bought in Asia or Europe to focus on finding similar ones in Brazil.

Sometimes we just read the Gazeta Mercatile, the *Wall Street Journal* equivalent in Brazil or the Folha de São Paulo, similar to the *New York Times*, to generate idea of companies to approach. We would look for stories of successful companies with strong management teams and start to think about the four ways we could create value. Debt to make leverage buyout investments in Brazil was not an option given the very high interest rates at the time. Reaching the owners of successful companies is not always easy. In those days, there really was not much private equity in Latin America and it was just starting to be more than just a cottage industry in the U.S., Europe and Asia. Venture philanthropy at scale is very much just a cottage industry today.

Simply put, scalable venture philanthropy is a service that exists to solve a challenge that large philanthropists have or may have, just like almost every investor on the planet has private equity investments as part of the alternative investments in their portfolios. Every financial advisor understands the science of reducing risk by diversifying a portfolio by including alternative investments like private equity, since their gains move in different directions than public markets. They will recommend anyone with even small amounts of funds to invest in uncorrelated investments so that when there are stock market drops, they can be protected by these investments that may be generating returns in the opposite direction. Our private investments into credit-card processors, private airports, cosmetic direct-marketing companies, software companies in Brazil, Mexico and Argentina often generated gains regardless of where public markets were moving.

Years later, as I looked at how to catch up every child in Palm Beach County, who can't read at third grade level by scaling The Salvation Army's local operation, I had to have a similar mindset and set of skills. How much can the revenue grow? Can costs be reduced somewhere to release some cash to grow? Can we borrow against our restricted endowed funds locally or nationally?

In the case of The Salvation Army, it was nearly impossible to find opportunities to reduce costs as they were incredible at being frugal, starting with the fact that their senior management are "officers," which are the equivalent to priests and ministers in their church. They are not compensated very much, nor do they own much except a remarkable and inspiring ability to dedicate their life to help others while expecting nothing in return. It was even hard for me to understand how they did not try to share their faith with others unless they had helped them over long periods of time and were asked why they did what they did. They are impressive servant leaders and most people I knew outside The Salvation Army did not know it is a church.

When I reached out to the owners of a company in Brazil at that time, it was often hard to see if they had $5 million or $50 million in revenue as there was no publicly available data or research on them. They did not have to file any reports with government regulatory agencies detailing their finances, disclosing who owned them or if they had any debt. Once we met with the owners or management, we could start piecing together a plan to see if our returns could be achieved. To do this, we would have to ask questions about past growth, future prospects, competitive pressure, supplier risks, industry dynamics, financial strength, debt risks and many other aspects that varied by industry. This was very interesting work, especially as it was not unusual that I would meet with five owners in five different industries every week, as mentioned.

Each company, owner, industry and country is different. They have different histories and risks. The quality of the management teams, their systems and their ability to create value are different. We used a concept of finding "deal killers" to help us discern quickly when to stop pursuing a possible investment since all we had was our time and reputation. We had $250 million in our first Latin American Fund that needed to be deployed. Although high returns were possible, losing some or all the fund was possible too. Especially investing dollar funds in countries with volatile currencies. We invested in private companies that were growing, where we hoped to also increase their profitability, increase their management strength and support them to be successful. Nevertheless, as mentioned, an unforeseen 30% movement in currency overnight could wipe out any returns permanently since our investments needed to be exited and the local currency converted to dollars in order to distribute gains to our clients.

As we look to solve our largest social and environmental challenges, a similar process is needed to deploy large philanthropy. The enormous funds that are available need to be gifted into nonprofits and invested into for-profits (private and publicly-traded companies). The reduction of risk is key. Venture philanthropy firms in the U.S. and globally have been doing this for 20 years. They have been backing nonprofit management teams, providing multi-year grants, bringing "more than just money" in terms of expertise in hiring senior management team members, board members, managing restricted assets, assessing legal risks and many other sophisticated advice, all while sitting on their Board of Directors, assuming fiduciary responsibility in the nonprofit. They are committed to the growth of the nonprofit and delivering transformative philanthropy to take these nonprofits to the next level.

This type of hands-on active management is at the heart of private equity, which, as mentioned, is an apprenticeship business as these skills of adding value need to be honed with experience. Especially those of helping organizations navigate crisis situations whether they be operating, financial, reputational or others. Venture philanthropy firms, some of which were created by private equity pros, are different than foundations or donors using venture philanthropy tools to improve their grant making. That is also critical. Adding data collection systems, funding the staff to run them effectively, analysing the data, reporting it and incorporating into a long-term growth plan are key to creating an actual solution. Incremental growth is excellent but solutions require organizational growth to the scale at which a problem can be solved. REDF, a venture philanthropy organization that looks to scale nonprofits that provide employment and training opportunities to men and women exiting prison in the U.S., for example, was started by George Roberts the co-founder of Kolberg, Kravis, Roberts (KKR), the most famous U.S. private equity firm.

As mentioned earlier, meeting private company owners in Brazil sometimes meant meeting three generations of family members in the first meeting. There was always curiosity and lots of scepticism by very successful businessmen being approached to purchase part or all of their companies. At the time, the term private equity was not part of the business lexicon. In Spain, at the time, the term "capital riesgo" was used, but in Brazil we just pronounced private equity with a Portuguese accent. The goal was to start a relationship and let them know the benefits of having a partner that was a respected global private equity firm.

I learned an important lesson in not making assumptions when I took a successful Brazilian entrepreneur to tour a company we owned in the U.S. that was in their same industry. It turned out the Brazilian company's operations were lightyears ahead of those of the U.S. company. Its whole warehouse system was automated while the one in the U.S. was not, despite being a much larger company. A relationship really was at the core of our successful work. Advent's Latin American team has been magnificently successful in the last 20 years. Building a great relationship based on integrity and transparency, never overpaying, knowing that the hard work started after we made an investment, diversifying across the region to mitigate currency, political and market risk, were all key to long-term success.

At a recent NextGen conference I was speaking at in Austin, I was asked about how nonprofits can go about finding the help to do these plans to entirely solve their cause. I said to them to find your local venture capitalists and ask them to help you answer the question of "how much" to solve a challenge in a community.

Venture philanthropy and scaling nonprofits or investing philanthropy into for-profit companies are all concepts that have existed for many years yet most people in the fields of nonprofits, foundations, philanthropy in general, wealth management, estate law and other related fields cannot explain what these are. We are still at an early point in the development of the venture philanthropy industry as a service provided to philanthropists to outsource their high impact giving. The advent of large venture philanthropy firms such as Blue Meridian Partners, Co-Impact and The Audacious Project are early movers in this service being offered at much larger amounts.

More organizations and private firms will continue to be created to provide this very value-added service. Donors will continue to pay for these services recognizing the work needed and value generated from their work. As larger amounts are allocated to them, more specialized talent can be hired from the private equity industry to more quickly increase impact and more efficiently reduce risk for philanthropists. We all benefit when risk is reduced and these fortunes are deployed with visible impact. Mistakes will be made, lessons will be learned, but as this industry develops as a new sector in asset management and fund management, more will see that the active management of large philanthropy has a valuable role. Philanthropists wanting to outsource their impact and enjoy the fulfilment generated by their generosity can benefit from the sophisticated skills of the venture philanthropists and the talent and dedication of the management teams delivering solutions.

Just like the wealthy outsource their other active investment needs to specialists (venture capital, later stage private equity, hedge funds, real estate and other alternative investments), they can now also start to outsource their large-scale, high-impact philanthropy. I believe future venture philanthropy firms should be for-profit entities since they are providing a valuable service and do not need to be supported by grants, instead of being set up as nonprofits. The more we incentivize those with the skills (due diligence, planning, structuring investments, supporting management teams, building partnerships) to apply these skills in helping philanthropists deploy more philanthropy, the better we all (including the planet) will be. These skills help ensure that the philanthropic investments have the highest probability of attaining scale.

There is a reason why venture capital and private equity firms, and other alternative investors like hedge funds, have had higher compensation than the managers of less active investing areas such as mutual funds and Electronic Traded Funds (ETFs) or the compensation of commercial lenders or foundation officers. They have specialized skills that are expensive to develop and the top performers have delivered high returns over decades which are uncorrelated to the markets. These returns are made in risky environments such as investing in private companies and a string of bad investments can end their careers. Their ability to choose the right investments, conduct extensive due diligence to find legal, accounting or other pitfalls before investing, their ability to consistently support management team and all the other skills represent real value that is added and translated into these uncorrelated returns with protection against market volatility.

"He who is controlled by objects
Loses possession of his inner self"
—Thomas Merton

11

Big Bets

I founded Merton in 2014 to help move large philanthropy into solutions. The earlier days of my work consisted of building large-scale growth plans for nonprofits, assuming (incorrectly) that if we built unique large-scale plans, donors would fund the projects. I thought The Giving Pledge Bottleneck was mainly caused because the signers of The Giving Pledge, and others wanting to give away mega-gifts, just weren't being offered opportunities to solve a whole challenge. While I found that those with the ability to finance the solutions to challenges were very interested in hearing about such an approach, getting them to commit funds was a longer process requiring longer-term engagement and meaningful relationships.

The philanthropists I look to meet are of two kinds. One is the early adopters of philanthropy innovation who have already funded or may be interested in committing funds to one of a handful of the large venture philanthropy groups. The other is what I call "frustrated philanthropists." These are the ones that had been giving large gifts every year to the local early learning or homeless nonprofit in which a solution never fully arrives. In many cases, the challenge is worse than ever. These philanthropists already have affinity to a management team at a nonprofit that could be scaled; they have the funds to greatly scale them and understand many of the complexities of the challenges on the ground.

Chuck Harris from Blue Meridian Partners warned me back then that most large philanthropists would be delighted to discuss scale issues but it would mostly be "happy talk" and that getting large philanthropists to actually commit funds would be wildly challenging. One of the greatest challenges

S. Davis, *Solving the Giving Pledge Bottleneck*, https://doi.org/10.1007/978-3-030-78865-0_11

for me so far has just been explaining the innovation that Blue Meridian Partners and their few peers are doing. Many senior foundation executives and sophisticated philanthropists have not yet heard of them, nor do they see how they are an important step towards the institutionalization of philanthropy and its resulting large flows into solutions. Most importantly, they don't know the volume of funds already being deployed. As a result, I have found myself sharing these exciting and necessary developments and suggesting that they, too, can outsource their philanthropy. Sharing their early success validates the process I'm advocating for as well. However, altering the approach for someone who has been doing philanthropy in the traditional way for decades is difficult and requires an "early adopter" mindset.

We need more groups looking to help large philanthropists identify and deploy their funds. I expect many to follow given it may be one of the largest opportunities to affect change in the world, as well as an opportunity to build profitable organizations who outsource this critical work for those who may want that value-added service. A few key philanthropists have built organizations of significant size like The Ballmer Group, Emerson Collective, Arnold Ventures, Chan Zuckerberg Initiative, Omidyar Networks and Virgin Unite, among others. These are hybrid groups acting as family offices that make both philanthropic investments and for-profit investments. Many of the other 2,825 billionaires[1] will not want to manage this themselves if they can outsource it to highly efficient and dedicated professionals. Yet keeping them engaged and experience the fulfilment of the impact they are making possible is key. Involving their children and other family members is also important as so many families have been unable to create what I refer to as "intergenerational philanthropic alignment," and this approach, when managed well, can generate that. Millennials and Generation Zs and their parents and grandparents all want to solve our greatest challenges. Scale can bring them together.

Charles Feeney, co-founder of Duty Free, built up a large team, while making sure it was ready to end its operations when they finished giving all of his philanthropy away through Atlantic Philanthropies. Their detailed reports named "Atlantic Insights" detail how they did it and are available to anyone free of charge. This advocacy is part of their spend-down strategy. His team knew it had a limited time. Atlantic Philanthropies provided a model for giving large grants in a few key areas, like higher learning, that were more in line with traditional philanthropy but in large enough amounts to actually spend down the $8 billion in his foundation. As he said "If you give while living, the money goes to work quickly and everyone gets to see the action and the results."[2]

Atlantic Philanthropies gave the grants across many countries including Australia ($368 million), Bermuda ($28 million), Cuba ($68 million), Northern Ireland ($570 million), Ireland ($1.3 billion), Vietnam ($382 million), South Africa ($424 million), the U.S. ($3.9 billion) and other global grants ($899 million).[3] Charles Feeney also made sure many of those countries' governments increased spending into what he was giving to in order to leverage their funds too. On the other hand, MacKenzie Scott has not seemingly built a team around herself, and this supports the idea of outsourcing large philanthropy.

The first Big Bet plan I developed over my first year after starting Merton was to greatly scale Community Partners, a local Palm Beach County, nonprofit with a $16 million budget. This makes it one of the largest social service nonprofits in South Florida. It had a well-respected management team that was led by Patrick McNamara, now CEO of Palm Health Foundation. As mentioned, Patrick was the only nonprofit CEO that had heard of Social Impact Bonds and had ties with national leaders who were thought-leaders in homelessness and children's services focused on overcoming trauma in poverty. Community Partners owned 83 permanent housing apartments for individuals who would otherwise be chronically homeless. They were very successful in providing services to them and keeping them housed. I approached Patrick with the concept of scaling his successful work by engaging large philanthropists in growth.

As mentioned previously, the scaling of Community Partners was a growth plan to add 500 permanent residences over ten years with $85 million in philanthropy. This would alleviate the crowding experienced in the eight local hospitals and save the State of Florida $7 million a year. These men who were sadly caught in a spiral of homelessness which saw them frequent emergency rooms, mental health services, jails and then go back to the streets. This is a national tragedy being repeated every day in every city in the U.S. Permanent housing with services where case managers help clients stay on top of their wellness, help them have jobs and be independent are badly needed.

Then, in 2017, I met with Carrefour, a nonprofit affordable housing developer in Miami that builds beautiful mixed-rent buildings with government tax credit grants. They have a similar approach to Community Partners in focusing on a Housing First model of providing permanent housing with services which aim for individuals and families to find stability quickly. Most of traditional homeless services provide short-term housing and focus on short-term stability. Yet, many of the complex issues of homelessness require long-term stability and mental health services to have any chance of success; therefore, permanent housing is key. Otherwise, the cycle of the "frequent users of the system" continues to play out with tremendous suffering and also at a high cost to our communities.

The game-changer of Carrefour for me was twofold: first, there is very large funding for every state readily available, albeit frequently in a competitive process. Both nonprofit and for-profit developers apply for federal funds through the Low-Income Housing Tax Credits (LIHTC[4]) which are run through each state and can provide $10 million or more in funding towards one specific housing project. So there was huge money, and it had been available for decades, yet no one in Palm Beach County had applied for it. Mostly, everyone had not known much about it or didn't have the dedicated resources to pursue the complex process of securing the funding. Carrefour had started doing projects outside of Miami-Dade County and opened its first modest Palm Beach County affordable housing project with 36 apartments in December of 2020.

Second, these buildings were entirely financially self-sufficient as they had a mix of long-term rents from firemen and teachers who would pay $1,200 a month for some apartments, while more vulnerable populations pay "deeply" affordable rates of $400 or $450 a month. Those in the latter category include people with serious disabilities, veterans with children and intense Post-Traumatic Stress Disorder (PTSD), or elderly couples on a fixed budget, all of whom would otherwise have to choose between buying their critical care medication, eating or being homeless.

So I realized there was significant funding available to build self-sufficient, beautiful affordable housing that wasn't being tapped. Buildings which didn't require additional funding are an incredible departure from most of the homeless shelters and short-term housing nationally which requires philanthropy and government grant money every year to pay for their operating expenses. Most of these residents leave these programs without tracking programs in place (again the funding and planning are not there) to see if they are successfully exiting homelessness. They also don't stay long enough to complete the application process to receive disability income or other sources of funds that can keep them housed permanently in this sustainable model.

The 500 men we were targeting in our Big Bet with Community Partners were chronically homeless, often veterans, with untreated mental health problems. Often just a few weeks of medication was all they needed to be very functional. Many of them had compounded their difficulties by having long-term untreated medical challenges and had incarceration histories, in large part from trespassing as they looked for places to sleep that were safer or warmer than being on the streets.

In 2020, we approached major national for-profit developers and created affordable housing deals which add philanthropy to existing LIHTC deals that are already approved. The goal is to replace debt with philanthropy. This approach will allow us to take nearly $500,000 in interest savings to reduce rents by that amount permanently. Thus, the percentage of apartments for vulnerable populations can go from 15% of the building to 45%. There are 1,000 buildings receiving LIHTC grants every year, and we estimate we could deploy about $3 billion in philanthropic funds annually just changing the capital structure and allowing us to improve the mix of apartments.

Since deeply affordable apartments are the most needed category of affordable housing, this is an example of deploying mega-philanthropy with great impact at scale. Both nonprofit and for-profit developers can do this and they are in a better position to be awarded these competitive grants if they do so. Local mayors are also enthusiastic to have more of these apartments in their communities rather than just mostly the higher rent ones. Some for-profit developers are able to provide the services needed to more vulnerable populations, and otherwise, our goal is to help them partner with nonprofit providers locally as part of our value-added philanthropic impact approach. Philanthropists get to fund impact at scale with the largest and most efficient national affordable housing developers, which can take in as much philanthropy as we can provide.

The real game-changing impact comes when philanthropists are willing to help us and developers and nonprofit partners be more proactive and target specific populations for solutions. Mega-philanthropy can simply augment the limited funds available annually under LIHTC cycles, with a new building possible with an additional $10 million in philanthropy, depending on the number of units and location. This is a real game changer as we can add 10 buildings per city. We can look at solving many related challenges as housing is the most capital-intensive piece in delivering solutions. As discussed, the vast majority of homeless services, foster care and the fight against human trafficking are short-term stabilization services without the long-term solutions. Therefore, millions trudge every day in every city in America between the streets, jails, hospitals and cash-strapped nonprofits and government service providers. It is important to reiterate that the men and women who work for these organizations are very committed and dedicated to providing excellent services but they are under water simply due to a lack of capital that would meet the needs of the people in front of them.

Blending large philanthropy to better leverage affordable housing already in development and targeting solutions not currently being pursued is the way forward and the way to encourage more government funding to become available after showing success. Carrefour and the affordable housing players focusing on the homeless have an annual retention rate higher than 85%. Some as high as 96%. This is the solution for the homeless housing crisis.

An example is to target the 200 women with children sleeping in their cars tonight in each of thousands of American cities and communities. LIHTC funds for one building in an area can be replaced by $10 million in philanthropy per building which developers would love to build more of. We would then add another $10 million in philanthropy to have the building support 45% deeply affordable apartments, versus the traditional 15%. Building just two more 300 unit buildings with an additional $40 million in philanthropy (half would replace LIHTC funds as they are limited in number by geography) would generate enough beautiful, self-sufficient mixed-rent housing to fully solve this challenge in one location permanently. Of course, 55% of the building also relieves some of the regular affordable housing pressure in any community.

The developers are delighted to build two more and they make the same return in our model than the typical LIHTC deal. A similar amount could house the youth ageing out of foster care in every community where they usually become homeless. Rolling these out across 100 cities would require about $4 billion in philanthropy. That is a little more than 0.7% of the 2022 Giving Pledge commitments estimate.

The goal is to continue co-investing philanthropy with affordable housing developers in for-profit projects until all the affordable housing for vulnerable populations is reached nationally. The plan is to grow our team of executives experienced in real estate investing to engage the largest developers to do so, while attracting the philanthropy. This will all be done on a profitable basis where even nonprofits can be contracted to provide services complementing the housing. We would still be at less than 10% of The Giving Pledge's amount estimated for 2022. Elon Musk alone could provide all the philanthropy needed to meet all the housing needed for vulnerable populations in this way if he gave half of his pledge based on his reported wealth as of January 2021 of over $200 billion.

The $85 million Community Partners growth plan also contemplated the first philanthropy funded Social Impact Bond. Most of the hundreds of Social Impact Bonds and similar contracts are meant to pilot an intervention that saves a government money. They are services governments could be providing but are not. So investors are offered the opportunity to make a profit and do good. The funds are given to a nonprofit to scale their work and track the cost savings to the government, which has agreed to pay the investors back their investment and a 7% or so return. Our logic was that if we could use large philanthropy instead of investor money, all government payments would flow back to the nonprofit and help make it sustainable. More recently, this has been done in a similar way by signing performance contracts where governments pay nonprofits directly for their work. This also avoids the expensive cost of setting up Social Impact Bonds.

The mixed-rent housing approach is even better, as the buildings are profitable and therefore fully sustainable. Given the extreme demand for affordable housing, they are oversubscribed and always full. Co-investing large philanthropy with for-profit players that can deliver the buildings in large numbers and operate them efficiently is a better model than our first Big Bet. We don't have to worry about the added pressure of a much larger operation for a nonprofit, or upgrading their systems, adding to their management teams, or building a larger development effort to raise more funds.

The Community Partners growth plan was completed in 2016. I shared the plan widely in my network and pitched it to several philanthropists and foundations. My goal was to secure the first $10 million gift into a DAF that would make the initial gifts to Community Partners according to our growth plan. One of the challenges was that almost the entire Community Partners budget was derived from government grants and so they didn't have major donors that would make this first gift. This proved a much bigger challenge than I imagined. Many of the philanthropists loved the approach and the scale, and yet getting them to commit was hard. One of the prospects I approached was Henry "Budge" Jamison who is a friend and was the Chairman of the local chapter of The Salvation Army.

Budge and I discussed the Community Partners scale-up and he said that he wouldn't fund it but that he did want me to develop a Big Bet for The Salvation Army. This had many advantages including that they would pay me, unlike Community Partners. Although I did have to join them as their Development Director in order to lead the large growth plan, it was attractive as I was going from Community Partners which was a local nonprofit with no major donors to one of the most recognized and admired global nonprofits with hundreds of thousands of donors. The Salvation Army in Palm Beach County was about a $12 million a year operation across many services including homeless housing and services, prisoner re-entry housing, community centers, youth programs, education programs and many others.

The Salvation Army is an impressive organization. The dedication of its officers and staff was incredible. Who drives feeding trucks towards Category 5 hurricanes? The spirit of those at "The Army" was also hard to put into words as they stretched every dollar and encouraged every volunteer to go a little farther than seemingly possible. They also didn't preach or try to evangelize those they served unless those receiving the help got to the point of wondering and asked them why they did it. It was very inspiring.

With $3.3 billion[5] in U.S. annual budget and about $4 billion in global annual budget, and with about $8 billion in U.S. restricted funds that generate about $500 million in annual interest to fund just the U.S. operations, The Salvation Army is able to cover much of the globe and provide admirable services. They are very much both a traditional nonprofit and very innovative in some ways including being a leader in transgender homeless housing. As the local development director, I had my full-time job of raising funds and also being the person in charge of communications during disasters. I did have a team of eight full-time employees and consultants to get more done. They had already hired consultants to create a local strategy and had the foresight to hire for-profit consultants who were quick to assimilate my Giving Pledge Bottleneck concept and the opportunity to develop a Big Bet.

After spending a year focusing on LIHTC projects and partnering with Carrefour to pursue a grant, it was clear that early learning may be a better fit for The Salvation Army. We had become lost in the huge Salvation Army approval bureaucracy for a new housing approach that was so much more attractive and effective, so we concluded we should focus on scaling their early learning program which would require no such approvals in regional or national offices.

We studied the Utah early learning social impact bond and developed a plan to add enough teachers, buses and buildings over ten years so that no child would reach the third grade behind in reading in Palm Beach County. What resulted was a plan to extend the current services across the county to cover 5,000 children a year that were behind. The total was 7,000 a year but we knew there were those with more specialized help that were outside our immediate scope, and whom we would incorporate later.

Our plan included adding significant systems, staff, middle management and senior management to handle the growth and the increased fundraising needs. It also included a philanthropic social impact bond based on a social impact bond in Utah[6] where a portion of the $2,000 in cost savings per child was paid back to investors. The Utah program was a great success, yielding $10 million in cost saving for the state and leading to the state taking over funding given its effectiveness. This was the ideal outcome that Social Impact Bonds were created to fulfill. In our case, we aimed to fund the social impact bond with philanthropy rather than with investor funds that would eventually exit the system. Thus, The Salvation Army would receive those success payments, increasing our sustainable revenue so we wouldn't be completely dependent on donors as our annual budget grew from $12 million to $80 million over ten years.

This was Merton's second Big Bet growth plan. I remember sharing the $176 million plan with the education team of a major national foundation. They were impressed with the scale of the effort and had never seen a plan to solve an entire educational challenge in a geographic area. All of the Big Bet plans we did also included the details of our 10-year expansion so that donors could study our assumptions including detailed investments in management, systems and assets. Plans like these are extremely rare in the nonprofit world and for good reason. Until The Giving Pledge, the possibility of large funds to fully solve a challenge was generally inconceivable. Our plan was also built 100% on nonprofit delivery in a "hub and spoke" strategy thus avoiding the school district and any politics.

At the end of the day, we saw a similar fate at The Salvation Army. Converting someone from a $1,000 a year gift to $10,000 gift was possible but larger gifts proved more difficult. Our local board was sincerely interested in growth and had the desire to reach out to the very wealthy in Palm Beach and Jupiter Island to find our first $10 million or more, yet those introductions never materialized. "If you build it they won't come," was proving itself true even if there were donors, well-meaning board members, a great brand and a very unique plan with the most scale and impact nationwide. Nevertheless, we also created the first entire solution to a major social challenge that we could find.

Finally, there was a third plan that surprisingly went unfunded given that this nonprofit only had three donors and each was a billionaire. Purpose Built Communities in Atlanta had a successful model to turn around bleak neighborhoods in America which was a concept I didn't know was possible. Tom Cousins, Warren Buffet and Julian Robertson fund the $5 million annual budget of Purpose Built. Purpose Built provides free consulting to cities who want to bring the model and adapt it to their location. It is widely considered as the leading model in place-based initiatives, bringing multiple resources to a defined area to effect great change over a ten-year period.

As discussed earlier, a bleak neighborhood could receive simultaneous investments in a cradle-college school, a community center and new mixed-income housing, all to attract low-income families into the neighborhood and begin a renewal. I designed a $100 million expansion with the view of raising funds that would be very impactful and would accelerate over 20 neighborhoods that were already in process. None had reached maturity which was needed to prove the case outside of their original success in their East Lake turnaround in Atlanta. It struck me that a more centralized management of funds and the creation of a national group of developers, nonprofits and donors could help scale the neighborhoods and start many others. To date, each neighborhood was independently organized and financed, and if money was available, it should be deployed in more scalable way.

Given that each neighborhood takes about $300 million to be "turned around," and that East Lake was successful in many ways, including in property values increasing over 300% in 12 years, there is a great argument for scaling their initial success, continue to prove it with the next 20 and then take this approach to the 825 most bleak neighborhoods in America. This is a path to raise the 10 million who suffer most from inter-generational poverty in the U.S. What could be more impactful than this? There are many organizations engaging in place-based initiatives and Purpose Built is a unique and admired model. Beyond our strategies at Merton to purchase distressed water utilities to bring clean water to the 21 million Americans who lack it, and to greatly scale the deployment of affordable housing, a large-scale strategy to turn-around these neighborhoods would also be one of the largest actionable social justice opportunities for mega-philanthropy.

One of the challenges is that efforts should be mostly locally-led and include all the different residents, and their histories there, in order to really be successful. This is not easy and Purpose Built spends two years developing this without imposing anything from above. This ultimately is what prevented our plan from being presented to the board and the donors. Purpose Built is an outstanding leader in this space and acts as an independent consultant that is there to assist but not to drive the process. As I looked forward to how to make this scaling happen, I realized we needed to be a third-party investor of philanthropy, bringing capital and expertise across all neighborhoods, rather than trying to scale the nonprofit consulting company into being something they are not.

Overall for Merton, the strategy of "if you build it, they will come" did not work between 2014 and 2019. Over the same period, the first large venture philanthropy teams (Blue Meridian Partners, Co-Impact, The Audacious Project and others) were rising in the world of philanthropy. They had each started with the funds and had a group of billionaires or large foundations working together, from the outset, to fund their projects and develop a new model of delivering larger philanthropy to scale nonprofits. Some of these early innovative billionaires funded several or all of these. They recognized they needed multiple groups of active managers to do the hard and detailed work of scaling nonprofits. This was similar to their personal portfolios where they had many active managers in each of their alternative investment buckets (venture capital, private equity, hedge funds).

We also realized we had to start with the large funders, and not the projects. As I shifted my approach and started looking for the first "anchor donor" for our work, I also found a different approach to scaling nonprofits with Big Bets. It was much more compelling to blend large philanthropy into for-profits than to scale nonprofits to solve our largest social and environmental challenges. These became more obvious and more pronounced the more I explored them starting the summer of 2019. This approach came out of a need to find donors, not as a result of thinking about this in a vacuum. I had started to reach out to former private equity mentors and colleagues for funding as many of them were strong candidates for mega-gifts given their investment success and having built large successful firms over the last 20 or 40 years.

First was the realization that together the most scalable nonprofits today could only take in 5% of The Giving Pledge commitments. As explained earlier, there aren't that many nonprofits able to quickly scale their operations with $200 million over 10 years. If we assumed there are 150 such nonprofits and we could scale all of them with $200 million that would be a total amount of $30 billion. A huge amount but only 5% of The Giving Pledge funds estimated of $600 billion by 2022.[7] Of course, any nonprofit would gladly accept $200 million, possibly endow the funds or explore ways to use the funds, but few nonprofits are ready to develop and run with a detailed ten-year plan to greatly scale at a much more aggressive rate than ever before.

Second, most nonprofits may have culture and management challenges that may prevent the type of incredible change expected in large scalings. As mentioned previously, the nonprofit sector has been starved for management resources due to the Overhead Myth and its pressure to greatly limit their ability to invest in management training, planning and systems. These are key requirements before they can scale quickly. This could take much time and difficult management changes may also need to be made, which could create conflicts at the board and staff levels. Many nonprofits are designed to be good stewards of resources and can be very fiscally responsible but are not necessarily designed to change quickly.

I saw this first-hand at The Salvation Army, where employees had been in roles for many years and the thought of change, or bringing in new people, or entering other areas of work was met with resistance at the staff level but also at the state and regional levels. There were many previous attempts to initiate change that had died in the bureaucracy designed to be fiscally responsible, and in some cases rightfully so. Even in one of the largest and leading nonprofits, change was hard to initiate and accomplish.

The Salvation Army also prides itself in spending only about 18% of their income in management and fundraising. Although this is virtuous in the world of traditional philanthropy, it starves it of the ability to attract managers with more sophisticated skills and to invest in the kind of planning we did in Palm Beach County. Change in a large nonprofit can be like turning a tanker, requiring much effort and time. Even some nonprofits that Blue Meridian Partners is scaling with $200 million had to do great work to be ready to scale.

On the other hand, smaller nonprofits are more nimble but may also need to make significant changes in order to scale at the levels that Blue Meridian Partners is doing. In a way, scaling nonprofits can be similar to restructuring private equity investments, where significant changes need to take place at the same time that growth is being pursued. It is the proverbial fixing the plane's engine in flight. Smaller nonprofits may also not have the depth of management and programs and operations staff to double in size in the near term. Rapid growth can seem appealing but can create serious operational and financial issues. From the point of view of fundraising, a larger organization means a larger development machine is needed to keep up with increased expenses. Some of this may be in the form of endowed funds, while some in the form of a larger major gifts team.

As the larger venture philanthropy organizations have discovered, coming to an end of a five- or ten-year grant period creates an "exit" problem. Venture capital and private equity firms are always looking for an exit from their investments so they can realize their gains for investors and raise a new fund. This is how they stay in business. Larger venture philanthropy provides gifts that represent a much larger portion of an organization's annual budget than other gifts. When these end, it can hurt the organization. Some of the first venture philanthropy firms that have been making value-added gifts to nonprofits are operating at the venture level. A $500,000 gift can be assimilated more easily than a $200 million gift. One Big Bet of $200 million can total the same dollars of all the giving over 20 years of some of the traditional venture philanthropy firms. It is clearly critical that larger venture philanthropy firms pursue exits carefully and prepare the organizations they are scaling to continue to grow without them.

The risk of creating larger organizations that are not sustainable is real, yet they can be mitigated. Government performance contracts are providing a path, where a nonprofits' services are remunerated by local and state governments providing ongoing revenue to replace the large contributions that come to an end. Over the next 5 years, we will see if Blue Meridian Partners, Co-Impact, The Audacious Project and others are successful in deploying the funds they set out to give on behalf of donors, and how much and how well the organizations they have backed have scaled. A key determinant will be the sustainability these organizations attain so that they can continue to move towards solving the challenges these Big Bets are being designed to move nonprofits towards.

Notes

1. The Billionaire Census 2020, Wealth-X, https://www.wealthx.com/report/the-wealth-x-billionaire-census-2020/.
2. Atlantic Insights, Giving While Living, Page 12, The Atlantic Philanthropies.
3. Atlantic Insights, Operating for Limited Life, Page 35, The Atlantic Philanthropies.
4. The Low-Income Housing Tax Credit - How It Works and Who It Serves, Corianne Payton Scally, Amanda Gold, Nicole DuBois, Urban Institute, July 2018.
5. The Salvation Army, 2020 Annual Report, www.salvationarmyannualreport.org.
6. Deseret News, Paying for success: The story of how Utah became a leader in social impact investing, Emily Hoeven, February 8, 2019, https://www.deseret.com/2019/2/8/20665405/paying-for-success-the-story-of-how-utah-became-a-leader-in-social-impact-investing.
7. A billionaire who signed The Giving Pledge in 2012 said Bill Gates' philanthropy pact isn't 'growing as rapidly as we hoped,' Business Insider, Taylor Nicole Rogers, October 24, 2019, https://www.businessinsider.com/billionaire-signed-giving-pledge-isnt-growing-rapidly-as-hoped-2019-10#:~:text=The%20Giving%20Pledge%20could%20be%20worth%20%20%24600%20billion%20by%202022&text=The%20pledge%20now%20has%20204,research%20firm%20Wealth%2DX%20found.

"We awaken, not to find an answer absolutely distinct from the question, but to realize that the question is its own answer"
—Thomas Merton

12

Pitfalls in Scaling Nonprofits

Dan Pallota changed the nonprofit world in a few significant ways. He pointed to critical faults in the nonprofit world that were obvious but had never been pointed out in quite the same way. He delivered a Ted Talk on May 11, 2013, titled, "The Way We Think About Charity Is Dead Wrong"[1] which has been watched over 5 million times. Since then, he has gone on to do countless speaking engagements and has published several books which highlight one simple idea: we have starved the nonprofit world of the resources needed to grow and thus solve the challenges they were created to tackle.

Dan clearly lays out the most challenging part of running a nonprofit: you are expected to operate with minimal resources, taking on daunting daily difficulties, you are not rewarded for taking on more, while at the same time being penalized for investing in the necessary management or systems. There has been a constant and overwhelming pressure on nonprofits to operate and be evaluated by what Dan called the "Overhead Myth." The idea that we fail to evaluate nonprofits on their impact, growth capabilities and quality of their work, because we are mostly focused on how much they spend on their overheard. Their overhead is defined as dollars spent on management and fundraising within the total annual budget.

What has resulted is immense pressure for nonprofits to avoid investments in their management and their systems. As mentioned previously, in my work with The Salvation Army, I saw how many of the staff had to have multiple jobs to make ends meet, as the salaries of nonprofit employees can be the lowest in any profession. I have been involved in nonprofits as a development officer, as a member of their Board of Directors, or as a venture philanthropy advisor, and in most of them, I have seen the pressure to not invest in systems that can save money in the short- to mid-term, as the immediate overhead ratio could be too high and result in great criticism and lower gifts.

As a result, nonprofits cannot make all the investments they need to be more efficient and effective such as the human talent needed to create a multi-year growth plan, invest in the development professionals that can bring more funds in, pay for the systems that better track donors and identify those major donors they should focus on, and countless others to be able to move towards solving problems.

Dan's work resulted in Charity Navigator and Guidestar, the two most reputable rating companies for nonprofits, to issue open letters saying that using the overheard ratio was not the way nonprofits should be evaluated. He points out that charities that had a 20% overhead ratio or less were considered excellent and worthy of donations. And the lower the overhead ratio, the more the worthiness. A low overhead ratio today is central to the fundraising pitches of most nonprofits. And the higher the overheard ratio, the more the management should be chastised for being inefficient. Dan clearly pointed out that a bake sale with a 5% overhead ratio was very efficient but only raised $100. An excellent fundraising program could have a ratio of 30%, especially if investing in marketing to draw people in and raise $100 million. Which one is better to fund solutions to our most pressing environmental and social challenges?

The overhead ratio goes against everything we know about being successful in any business. Spending more than 30% on management and marketing is necessary for many businesses. But it is not acceptable for nonprofits. Clearly, it is key to attract the best people and set up the best systems. It is important to invest in growth in order to grow. On the other hand, it is hard to evaluate nonprofits if they aren't growing and if they don't have the systems to track anything except outputs such as how many of the children they serve attended their after-school programs. Some larger nonprofits have made investments in systems and can track outcomes, such as how many of those children had their grades increase by 10% or more in their program and sometimes nonprofits have the specialized systems and employees to measure the impact that these outputs and outcomes have had on their communities. These can be things like the long-term cost savings to the city, or state, from increased graduation rates and increased employment. True impact measurement is rare as it requires significant investments which bump up against the pressure of the dreaded overhead ratio.

Another pervasive challenge to getting nonprofits the management and system investments they need to succeed is the related and also fear-based and short-sighted focus some donors have in demanding that their funds only fund programs. In other words, they are saying that they don't want any of their money to fund overheads. Given the nature of nonprofits, and how they have to focus on attracting donors and building relationships with them, there is an attitude of having to be satisfied with what donors are willing and able to give to them. This creates much uncertainty and leaves nonprofits facing massive funding challenges.

Restricting donor gifts to programs can greatly cripple nonprofits. The fear is that nonprofits will be overpaying their staff, something that has been widely reported in a few tragic cases of abuse. But the vast majority of nonprofit managers are underpaid and continue to manage the nonprofits they lead with miniscule management resources and almost no efficient systems. Ironically, this makes them less capable of making an impact. This philosophy of "I just want my money to reach the clients" or "be used for programs" creates even larger problems in that the management teams were already overwhelmed and now have to run more programs with the same strained resources. Nonprofits need to be able to invest more in management, marketing, and systems. That is how growth works.

I remember as a development officer I struggled to invest in systems that would save us money. We didn't have much planning capability to even justify the investments. Intergenerational changes have also made this dynamic more complicated. Philanthropy was moving from donors having a "Greatest Generation" outlook of giving gifts with few strings attached where they trusted the nonprofits to make the best decisions given their acute needs, to Baby Boomers who wanted to see the numbers and the outputs, yet not necessarily make the investments to clearly report these. We wanted to keep better track of our data, have someone we could hire that was dedicated to that very time-consuming work, produce meaningful reports for donors, create plans that projected the details of fundraising campaigns for programs and buildings and to be able to show donors that we could take a bigger bite out of the problem.

Yet, we were constantly being told by donors to, "just do what you can," while being expected to do the job of three people at once. How could we do any one job well? The following generation of millennials wanted to support different charities with less long-term commitment, give online and also see very specific impact and solutions in the short-term. Adapting somewhat to these changes was possible, yet doing so on a constant shoestring budget greatly frustrated staff and morale. Still, these additional donor requirements for outputs, outcomes and impact did not come with increased funding to pay for the detailed work to quantify and report these.

Fear of nonprofits spending too much on salaries continues to fuel the gravitational pull of the overhead ratio and the focus on funding everything but management costs. There is a similar parallel in the U.S. with taxes that create a brutal lack of funding. There is a fear that the tax funds will be wasted because the government cannot be trusted to solve social or environmental issues effectively. While I'm sure there are many examples of this taking place, I also know that there are great government programs that do work. But as we cut back on taxes, as a perceived virtue, we continue to starve solutions. As government expenses are reduced, nonprofits are expected to fill-in the gap.

This is similar to the fear mentality that has also hurt corporate philanthropy, where boards, especially in the past, would not want to fund more philanthropy. The view was that the purpose of the corporation was to maximize shareholder value and that philanthropy should be left for each shareholder to decide on their own. So this was yet another force to reduce philanthropy.

As mentioned earlier, in the summer of 2016, I was invited to teach a group of Austrian MBAs that were studying at Palm Beach Atlantic University in West Palm Beach. As I presented topics on innovative homeless housing solutions, they listened quietly. I walked them through Social Impact Bonds and how I was working on my first Big Bet with Community Partners to house 500 of the chronically homeless in the county who regularly used the homeless shelters, the jails and the emergency rooms, and thus were referred to as "frequent users." The approach was innovative in scale, in using detailed 10-year planning, but also in using philanthropy to fund the social impact bond. So rather than using investor funds where success payments exited the system, payments would go to the nonprofit to reach sustainability. I was very enthusiastic, explaining how we could put $85 million in philanthropy to work and save the State of Florida $7 million a year in cost savings from these individuals not arriving at the county's emergency rooms, homeless shelters or jails.

The students remained quiet and they began to seem confused. I started to think that I had been spending too much time on the "how" rather than creating the right context of the "why" to really capture their hearts. Instead of moving on, I found out what the issue was. One of them raised their hand and said, "why don't you just raise taxes and house them all?"

I was baffled as I had never had to explain this to American students. All I could say was that we disliked paying taxes. In fact, it had become common to believe that paying less in taxes was a virtue. Very careful spending of tax money is a virtue. Averting situations where taxes are not spent efficiently and effectively is key. These students were right in pointing out the obvious that the real reason there was so little housing and services for the homeless was that we would not raise taxes as a community to take care of them. And yet the costs of not taking care of them were much higher. This was the whole premise of our Big Bet. We could encourage philanthropists to fund our large expansion, with very visible impact and we would track the cost savings to the state government to encourage them to fund the ongoing additional expenses to continue to lock in their cost savings. But I had to recognize that the same expansion in housing and related services could be funded by $85 million in new taxes, and it would quickly pay for itself.

This is an example of the consequences of a deeply underfunding nonprofit and government social services in America today. Merton's work is to create vehicles to deploy mega-philanthropy using for-profits as vehicles for impact at scale. These will encourage more government spending to upgrade America's infrastructure and have more affordable housing for the most vulnerable populations. All this creates stronger communities.

It was clear that the commitment and dedication of the government employees in Palm Beach County that were tasked with overseeing homelessness were very high. They too suffered from a dire lack of resources to invest in planning in order to have a plan that would be considered excellent in the for-profit world. Much of the planning work was expected to be done in addition to their full-time job, which in many cases left them doing three jobs instead of just one.

Overall, the individuals at nonprofits that I have worked for have been willing to work harder for less on a daily basis. The dedication of these teams was clear and grounded in their deep calling to do good and take on our societies' deepest, darkest, most difficult and most neglected problems. Seeing homeless individuals trust our case managers, begin to take medication and act like completely different people, who were stable and some even joined our staff, was nothing short of witnessing regular miracles. Seeing them come back to show us the keys to their new home or to share stories of their jobs was incredible. Homelessness has solutions and the homeless housing crisis is solvable leveraging for-profit developments with mega-philanthropy.

And yet there was no scale. As I looked across the U.S., there are large nonprofits, but they too seem to stall in terms of growth and resources. Even those that have miraculously attained great scale, have long-term financial resources in the form of endowments and have some ability to market and continue to deliver services are only meeting a small percentage of the need for their causes. They also struggled to raise the funds they need in every region of the country in which they operated to keep the lights on, let alone to grow towards a solution. According to Bridgespan, only 144 of the 200,000 nonprofits started since 1970 had reached $50 million in revenue.[2]

The great challenge for nonprofits is the lack of planning and the disconnect of what that means with business leaders on their boards and with donors. It is very rare to see a nonprofit with a multi-year budget, let alone a detailed 10-year budget, even if it is just a projected income statement. This is the minimum a for-profit company would consider as a "plan." This is a document used to plot the long-term course of an organization which shows different scenarios given different choices that can be pursued. It shows the future funding necessary to attain the goals of these scenarios and makes possible the productive planning discussions necessary to refine plans with inevitable future challenges and opportunities.

Given that nonprofit management teams are constantly underwater from a resources point of view, and each individual employee is expected to do three jobs, there is no surprise that detailed long-term planning is elusive. If you are trying to keep the lights on today, and are relying on key annual grants or major gifts to get there, planning several years out seems like a luxury that cannot be had. Hence, nonprofits are left with developing "strategic plans" that many times are the result of an all-day meeting with senior staff and outside advisors. They are focused heavily on developing the right mission and vision of an organization. They list ideas of areas to tackle in the new year, but they tend to be very qualitative and short on numbers. So given how we have starved nonprofits for resources, especially planning, it is not surprising that most of these strategic plans are neither strategic, nor are they "plans" relative to their for-profit equivalents.

Venture philanthropy firms have led the way to begin to improve these challenges by providing multi-year grants, instead of having nonprofits start each year from zero. They have also been helping nonprofits redefine their planning, which involves investing in key areas such as management training and systems. The planning, like many key parts of life, becomes the answer to the question of "how much?"

Notes

1. Dan Pallota, TED Talks, The way we think about charity is dead wrong, March 11, 2013, https://www.ted.com/talks/dan_pallotta_the_way_we_think_about_charity_is_dead_wrong.

2. How Nonprofits Get Really Big, William Foster & Gail Fine, Stanford Social Innovation Review, Spring 2007, https://ssir.org/articles/entry/how_non profits_get_really_big.

"When humility delivers a man from attachment to his own works...he discovers that perfect joy is possible only when we have completely forgotten ourselves."
—Thomas Merton

13

Institutionalizing Philanthropy

Since founding Merton Capital Partners and entering large venture philanthropy work, I have been looking for partners or clients that understood the importance of creating vehicles to deploy The Giving Pledge commitments. I have had many conversations with large wealth management firms, and many smaller ones, as well as with several Donor Advised Funds and many types of philanthropic advisors. I suspected that some wealthy individual families and individuals were asking these, especially their financial advisors, for larger philanthropic suggestions. I believe many, many more will follow in the footsteps of MacKenzie Scott and her ground-breaking gifts in 2020 and 2021, and also accelerate the increases in their giving.

Most of the large wealth management firms also have philanthropy teams to help clients think through their philanthropy and keep them up to date on philanthropic trends. I have had several discussions with members of these teams and the impression I have is that their main goal is to reinforce the relationships between the bank and their clients but not necessarily to help them be proactive with giving away larger amounts. There is of course a basic conflict in that wealth management teams are mostly compensated by fees charged based on each client's assets under management (AUM). So why would a financial advisor be interested in helping their clients make larger gifts that reduce their AUM when that would directly reduce their personal compensation? The name of the game is asset gathering and teams are measured and paid by how much they manage.

Having said that, from a corporate point of view, philanthropy is the largest pool of unmanaged funds in the world requiring active managers. It is the fastest way for wealth management firms to generate very large, measurable and visible social impact for themselves and their clients. They have large foundations that already give funds away and some will "co-invest" their gifts with that of clients. This is not the traditional corporate matching giving program for bank employees. These are corporate foundations actively looking to have impact by helping create solutions for their client's philanthropic needs and giving alongside with them to have more impact. An excellent example is the UBS Optimus Foundation, which has played an active role in several world-leading initiatives to use their own philanthropy with more impact and to help clients do so as well. Some of the successful projects include several Development Impact Bonds (DIBs) such as Educate Girls, and the Quality Education India DIB.[1]

DIBs are similar to Social Impact Bonds (also referred as Pay-For-Success Contracts in the U.S.) where government funding to provide basic needs for communities is lacking and philanthropy steps in to prove and pilot new interventions with the hopes of governments buying into results and allocating greater funds to the innovative solutions. The first was set up in 2010 to reduce the recidivism rates in Peterborough prison in England. It was led by a group including Sir Ronald Cohen, who is one of the founders of Apax Partners, the private equity firm based in London. Most of these types of performance-based contracts take investor funds looking to do good and make a profit, use the funds to increase the work of a nonprofit and have the government pay back the investors with a return once the impact and cost savings to the government are proven. Unlike Social Impact Bonds relying on governments to pay back investors, DIB investors are paid back by donors.

There will be movement towards wealth management firms partnering with large venture philanthropy firms, to offer their clients access to large impact projects. Donor will be able to fund detailed growth plans leading to solutions. Every nonprofit or for-profit tackling a social and environmental challenge needs to answer a simple question: "how much do you need to actually solve the challenge in your community or globally?"

Just because they don't have the answer today does not mean the data needed to calculate the number is not available. As discussed earlier though, the essential step is for these social entrepreneurs to attract venture capital and private equity specialists and not just take the data and put it into a spreadsheet to calculate the amount. They need to apply the basic private equity skills of evaluating the organizations and their management, looking at their growth prospects and financing challenges, and many others to refine such projections. Of most importance, of course, is the actual execution of the plans to scale the organization and generate the impact. For-profits do this daily everywhere in the world. Of course, the actual numbers will never be exactly the ones on the original plan. How can we present a large growth plan for donors to fund without these credible details? The good news is that every community has individuals with these skills.

Wealth management firms will be well served to partner with large venture philanthropy firms that can develop philanthropic investment opportunities for their clients. There is an additional disincentive for a wealth management financial advisor to encourage their client to make larger donations. If the client is dissatisfied with their gift to anything suggested by the financial advisor, this would endanger the relationship and thus their income. Of course, the financial advisor may wish the best for their client's giving, but there are real risks to encouraging larger philanthropy. Yet larger deployments into large projects like ours can be structured with DAFs to deploy funds and the AUM in the DAF can be managed by wealth management firms in the short-term.

My argument to the wealth management firms was that if we were going to be raising funds to be deployed into large impact opportunities, a wealth management firm would benefit in managing an ever increasing pool of gifts in a DAF, before they were fully deployed. This way they could target large prospects to give large gifts into our DAF and their AUM would in turn grow. It is also a great opportunity for them to approach large prospects with our innovative vehicles to deploy large philanthropy with great impact. As they build these relationships, they would benefit from larger AUM and they could obtain other parts of their investment portfolio to manage. At the very least, the latter would be a reason to call on large philanthropists that they didn't otherwise have access too.

This was not a strong enough argument to partner with them. We are not yet at the point where the process of deploying mega-philanthropy is institutionalized, but the conversations are being had and the questions are being asked. Soon, many of the same families that pressured their financial advisors to offer them higher rated ESG investments to replace companies in their portfolio that had poor ESG ratings will also pressure the same financial advisor to offer them the opportunity to make donations into situations that actually solve our social and environmental challenges. Clients demanding this is also the fastest way to move the large philanthropy that is on the sidelines into solutions.

The pain point that I've been looking to solve is that of donors who would like to get more funds gifted to actually solve our challenges, with measurable impact, but can't. Those that would welcome the ability to outsource the heavier more time-consuming work. Unlike just finding active managers to deliver returns like investors do with private equity, large venture philanthropy has an important difference. Donors are looking for fulfilment. The more visible and measurable the solution, the better. We all want to do good and move away from the current model of diffused impact in philanthropy today and more towards quantifying and funding specific solutions.

This will lead to higher levels of fulfilment and create value from dollars that would never be used, and thus have a low marginal value. Yet donor and family engagement also require specialized talent that can ensure the donors and their families participate in the solution as much as possible and in a way that is very positive and rewarding. This kind of client management work is specialized and key to incentivize more giving. There are few things as impressive to encourage others to give than a donor driven to share their enthusiasm with others.

The challenge is finding those early adopters that are not yet aware that they can fund the solution of a visible challenge. Donors are still left looking to give to charities the same way they always have. Venture philanthropy and their larger cousins need to greatly increase their public relations to raise awareness in the minds of future mega-philanthropists. Being able to outsource their giving into solutions with more fulfilment and at greater volumes is a great service.

I have found that individuals or families with significant philanthropy are each different and each has a different ecosystem of advisors helping them make their gifts. Sometimes it can be a single individual managing their foundation with no support staff. This individual can be part of the donor's family office, or, be a separate entity. It is not uncommon for wealthy donors to make gifts themselves and leave the administration of the foundation to their attorney or other trusted person. Of course, on the opposite side of the spectrum, you have foundations with hundreds of staff or you have sophisticated teams of gift and investment specialists at hybrid groups such as Virgin Unite, Omidyar Network, Arnold Ventures and The Ballmer Group.

These more sophisticated groups are not just making grants. They are investing in the whole spectrum of impact investing and in all the ways they can generate good, including by making returns. Some of these investments make a return as traditional for-profit investments, some are market-rate impact investments, and some are concessionary or catalytic investments which may be funded by philanthropy and return funds to their DAF or foundation. Finally, some are straightforward gifts such as those to a capital campaign of a school, university, church or local hospital.

Many philanthropists are also looking at generating a good by investing their gifts with impact while they are sitting at their foundation or DAF. The logic is that these pots of money have to be invested in order to generate the returns they need to continue to grow, pay out the minimum 5% required by the IRS (in the case of foundations) and cover all their costs including the staff of the foundation. In a traditional foundation portfolio, their wealth management firm would suggest a diversified portfolio comprised of a variety of short-term liquid investments, equities and bonds, and many types of alternative investments.

More and more there are mutual funds and ETFs focused on impact being used to replace traditional equity funds without an ESG focus. And in terms of alternative investments, there are venture capital and private equity managers specialized in impact investing. Thus, philanthropy can also be doing good while it is endowed or sitting in a DAF. Naturally, this also takes significant management time as making these investments for the corpus of an endowment or while they sit in a DAF is equally time consuming as they are exposed to losses. Automated impact investment options for DAF donors are increasingly common. But buyer beware, much due diligence is still required.

DAFs have also gotten much criticism despite having some simple and compelling benefits for donors. Rather than having to start a foundation which includes starting a corporation, applying for an IRS designation, filing 990 reports, employing lawyers and accountants and possibly staff, DAFs allow you to outsource all of that. So on the surface they are compelling tools for donors. It is simply opening an account at Fidelity Charitable where donors make their gifts and later ask the DAF to regift their funds to nonprofits with a simple phone call or email. These are "recommendations" but in essence are instructions as long as they fall into standard gifts. DAFs are 501(c)(3) organizations, and therefore, donor gifts are final and generate a tax benefit if the year of the gift to the DAF.

As DAFs have grown in size, it is estimated that there are almost $150 billion[2] in gifts from donors sitting in DAFs. Much of the criticism has been around there not being any requirements to gift at least 5% of their funds, as foundations must do annually. There is also criticism that the public cannot see where the gifts from the DAFs are ultimately given, unlike with foundations, where each gift is carefully listed and available online.

There is a practical argument to be made that often foundations are targeted heavily by unsolicited requests because their giving is public and nonprofits can gleen their philanthropic interests in the 990s of a foundation. DAF gifts to underlying nonprofits don't always reveal who the initial donor is. This is an additional benefit. Yet anonymity for one can be seen as undo secrecy to the next, especially as there is a tax benefit to the donor and thus calls for accountability are also understandable. For donors that manage most of their foundations on their own, receiving mountains of unsolicited requests is a real administrative burden. Using a DAFs skirts that issue.

According to the National Philanthropic Trust, net contributions to DAFs in their 2020 Donor Advised Report were over $39 billion in 2019. In that year, distributions or gifts recommended by philanthropists from their DAF accounts to underlying nonprofits were $27 billion. This represented a payout ratio of 22%. In terms of increase in giving, DAFs gave $12.4 billion in 2014 and $28 billion in 2019. During that year, new DAF accounts increased by 19%. It would seem that the giving rates of DAFs far exceed the 5% of foundations. Needless to say, it will be interesting to see how these debates unfold and if any changes to the structure of DAFs are mandated through legislation.

I have also had a few discussions with DAFs in order to partner with us to raise larger dollars from prospects they are targeting. I've had discussions about offering our vehicles to actually solve a large social issue like homeless housing in a particular county or a large environmental issue. To date, DAFs are more focused on raising funds and helping donors gift them from an administrative point of view but not to advise them as to where to give to, in a way drives scale in solving challenges. Soon, and this may have begun already, they will be working with the large venture philanthropy firms to channel large philanthropy in a more concentrated way.

Institutionalizing philanthropy is a win-win for philanthropists, wealth management firms, DAFs, the nonprofits, for-profits also receiving these funds and fundamentally those being lifted out of suffering with the funds. Our planet also needs these funds to flow. New sources of revenue are available for these firms, and they can in turn hire more talented professionals to finance the most good. The fulfilment that is possible for philanthropists is also real for all the players needed to fund and execute solutions. Joy for all is hard to deliver but very possible as we forget ourselves and focus on those in need and on the environment.

Notes

1. The Brookings Institution, Sarah Osborne and Emily Gustafsson-Wright, Thursday, December 17, 2020, https://www.brookings.edu/blog/education-plus-development/2020/12/17/the-worlds-largest-education-impact-bond-delivers-on-results-midway-through-the-program/.
2. The 2020 Donor-Advised Fund Report, National Philanthropic Trust, https://www.nptrust.org/reports/daf-report/.

"Love in fact is the spiritual life, and without it all the other exercises of the spirit, however lofty, are emptied of content and become mere illusions."
—Thomas Merton

14

The Other 95%

The excitement surrounding large venture philanthropy is obvious. They are deploying larger amounts of philanthropy and allowing a few nonprofits to greatly scale. After always operating from a position of scarcity, nonprofit leaders can start to see very large philanthropy being deployed and funding key needs required for rapid growth.

As new venture philanthropy organizations at scale like Blue Meridian Partners, Co-Impact, The Audacious Project and others like Lever For Change continue to grow, they will inspire others to provide this needed service to philanthropists, who we cannot expect to dedicate their lives to giving away the wealth they have accumulated. We need more organizations that act as an active manager of large philanthropy bringing groups of venture philanthropists together working directly with the management teams of the nonprofits they are funding to help them grow at faster rates.

As we look further into the horizon, we see that there is much more philanthropy available that can be deployed in the most scalable of nonprofits today. Given the historic limitations we have placed on nonprofits, namely penalizing them under the weight of the overhead ratio, there just are not that many nonprofits that can be scaled effectively with $200 million today. The large venture philanthropists are looking for nonprofits that are ready to scale rapidly in the short-term. Few have detailed 5- or 10-year plans. Blue Meridian Partners brings in BridgeSpan to help the nonprofit management teams of its future recipients of gifts to help build a plan, before beginning

S. Davis, *Solving the Giving Pledge Bottleneck*,
https://doi.org/10.1007/978-3-030-78865-0_14

to scale. And this can be a long-term process. The MacArthur Foundation relies on Lever For Change and other individual consultants to help their 100&Change competition finalists build detailed plans.

Many believe there are only a few nonprofits ready today to be scaled with $200 million in a way that its operations can take in the funds and grow in an efficient manner. There is also the issue of the "exit." What happens when the large venture philanthropy organization reaches the end of its grant making and the larger nonprofit now needs to replace that funding with that of others? Is a problem being created at the end? There are alternatives. In some cases, government contracts can come in to replace the grants in the form of earned revenue for services provided to the community.

If we are optimistic and assume there are 150 nonprofits that could be rapidly scaled with $200 million today, and we had more large venture philanthropy firms to round-up the donors and deploy their gifts, it would represent $30 billion over 10 years. This is an incredible amount of targeted philanthropy. Yet, as mentioned previously, it would represent only 5% of The Giving Pledge's 2022 estimated amount of $600 billion.[1]

Of course, 5% also does not consider the further growth in assets of The Giving Pledge signers or new signers coming in. More importantly, we have to remember that The Giving Pledge is made up today of about 200 signers. There are about 2,600 billionaires behind them and about 290,000 individuals and families with over $30 million in wealth globally.[2] Add to this corporate philanthropy looking for more scale to deliver "deeper" ESG impact. This means the pool of potential philanthropy that could be deployed to solve our world's largest social and environmental problems is very significant. Every day, the desire to do more good grows. The rising tide of good is creating demand for direct investing teams experienced in deploying philanthropy in a "hand's on" way and to ensure that impact can be attained and celebrated.

The good news is that even if we max-out on the nonprofits that can be scaled effectively in this new larger way, we can turn to for-profits to more efficiently and effectively deploy the other 95%. Philanthropy has been invested into for-profits for decades. Blended finance is the term for gifts that can be invested ("blended") into for-profits for a number of benefits, while furthering the mission of the donors and the exempt nature of their foundation. The IRS allows for gifts blended into for-profits if the purpose is to further a good a donor is pursuing. Donors can also use some DAFs, like ImpactAssets, to make similar blended investments.

The MacArthur Foundation made its first Program Related Investments (PRI) in 1983.[3] PRI are grants from a foundation that can be invested into a for-profit company (or a loan or guaranty) in the form of a security in order to further the foundation's mission rather than solely to generate an economic return. They are made from a foundation's annual payout (usually 5% of endowment is paid out). MacArthur has invested $517 million in 242 impact investments.[3] Yet only about 2% of the 87,000 foundations in the U.S.[4] use PRI. Foundations also make investments from their endowment, known as Mission-Related Investment (MRI). PRI originated in the U.S. Tax Reform Act of 1969.[4]

PRI generally generate both a financial and a social or environmental impact. There are many terms and structures that can be used depending on the specific situation of the investment. The Rockefeller Foundation formally launched its PRI program in the 1990s but has been making PRI since much earlier.[5] The Ford Foundation began its PRI program in 1968.[6] Today, the Bill & Melinda Gates Foundation has over $2.5 billion in PRI to further its mission, through its Strategic Investment Fund.[7] This is similar to a venture capital firm but using philanthropy to make the investments.

In some cases, gifts can be invested as a loan or as equity or as a hybrid. The funds can be "catalytic capital" that allows for a project to happen when otherwise it may not be financed. The investment can generate a return back to the foundation or DAF. The philanthropic investments can also be non-dilutive capital. In other words, the investment of philanthropy does not take an ownership stake in the for-profit company and thus does not participate in any economic gain. It is the equivalent of a grant allowing the project to take place and generating impact. Many PRIs aim at filling the gap that many global projects suffer from a lack of access to capital.

Other forms of blended finance include "first-loss" investments or loans meant to entice private investors to participate in a deal knowing that any initial losses will be covered by the philanthropy. This approach has been used in Social Impact Bonds and similar vehicles to also entice investors to participate by philanthropists insuring their investment or covering part of their losses. In the world of impact investing, philanthropy and capital invested on a for-profit basis by impact investors can also be "concessionary capital" where lower returns are accepted in order to also allow the deal to be completed. Deal structures also vary widely and are creative allowing philanthropy to be invested in for-profits while retaining certain rights as investors, even if donors (or government agencies and others) do not participate in the gains or even a return of principal.

As outlined by Jed Emerson in his book *The Purpose of Capital*,[8] philanthropists approach these investments with a sense of meaning, of furthering a mission and creating a good. Their individual mindsets will determine what investments, structures, rights and oversight they will have in their investing. These in turn will define the impact they will have on the social and environmental challenges they are looking to improve.

Another advocate of meaning and money is Paul Schervish, formerly with the Boston College Center of Wealth and Philanthropy (and a Merton Board of Advisor) who has written extensively on donors creating "moral biographies" to make sure that meaning is generated from their giving.[9] The etymology of philanthropy itself is from the Greek *philanthrōpos* meaning "loving-man."[10] Love of others is what generates the fulfilment that keeps us from a life empty of meaningful content. Our moral biographies are the change we have generated in the world with our work and our giving. As larger venture philanthropy firms are developed, and more make large deployments through investments in private deals, donor impact and this donor fulfilment will grow in exponential ways.

Notes

1. Wealth-X Billionaire Census 2020, Wealth-X, https://www.wealthx.com/report/the-wealth-x-billionaire-census-2020/.
2. Covid-19 Wealth Impact: The World Ultra Wealth Report 2020, Wealth-X, https://www.wealthx.com/report/covid-19-wealth-impact-the-world-ultra-wealth-report-2020/#downloadform.
3. Four Lessons from Four Decades of Impact Investing, May 8, 2018, MacArthur Foundation, https://www.macfound.org/press/40-years-40-stories/four-lessons-four-decades-impact-investing.
4. Program Related Investments: Why Aren't More Foundations Using Them?, Mary Ann Weiss, June 3, 2018, National Center for Family Philanthropy, https://www.ncfp.org/2018/06/03/program-related-investments-why-arent-more-foundations-using-them/.
5. Arabella Advisors, The Rockefeller Foundation's Program-Related Investments Portfolio—Final Evaluation, July 2013.
6. Supporting Economic Justice? Ford's 1968 PRI Experiment, Rachel Wimpee, November 1, 2019, Rockefeller Archive Center, https://resource.rockarch.org/story/supporting-economic-justice-fords-1968-pri-experiment/.
7. Bill & Melinda Gates Foundation, Strategic Investment Fund, https://sif.gatesfoundation.org/.
8. The Purpose of Capital, Jed Emerson, Blended Value Group Press, 2018.

9. Paul Schervish, "The Moral Biography of Wealth: Philosophical Reflections of the Foundation of Philanthropy," Nonprofit and Volunteer Sector Quarterly, Volume 35, No. 3, pp. 477–492, September 2006.

10. Merriam-Webster Dictionary, https://www.merriam-webster.com/dictionary/philanthropy.

"I must learn therefore to let go of the familiar and the usual and consent to what is new and unknown to me. I must learn to "leave myself" in order to find myself"
—Thomas Merton

15

Philanthropy in Clean Water Deals

In the summer of 2019, I was looking for partners and prospects to create vehicles to deploy The Giving Pledge commitments. Some of the ones I reached out to were retired private equity professionals I knew personally who have immense talent, as well as the funds to fund our first philanthropic deals. I spoke to several very successful professionals who were still active institutional investors, and some who had already retired. One was in the process of retiring and still in his mid-50s. I believed they would be attracted to how similar large venture philanthropy is to private equity work. They did appreciate how the private equity process had been adapted to philanthropy at the venture level by venture philanthropy firms. They had not heard of these firms but agreed that a similar process could be done at a much larger level, especially since the funds were seemingly available.

They also appreciated how more of the private equity process was needed as larger funds were put to work. This includes the same type of hands-on private equity processes for sourcing and evaluating opportunities, and due diligence to review operational, accounting and legal risks of scaling an organization. In the case of investing philanthropy with private partners in for-profit projects, we also want to negotiate the structuring of impact in the securities and have long-term active oversight of the investments to ensure impact is delivered. Similar to the classic private equity adage, large venture philanthropy looks to bring "more than just money" to the table in terms of value-added support of management and a focus on impact by setting specific impact milestones once the measuring and reporting capabilities are in place.

Private equity funds have limited partners, who include Ultra High Net Worth individuals (UHNWI) and not just pension funds, insurance companies and other institutions. I believe these individuals may also want

S. Davis, *Solving the Giving Pledge Bottleneck*, https://doi.org/10.1007/978-3-030-78865-0_15

similar active investing help to deploy their philanthropy with more scale and impact.

I reconnected with Alex Loucopoulos, who is a partner at Science Water. Alex is an old friend from Georgetown University's School of Foreign Service, and he too went on to J.P. Morgan's investment banking program in New York after graduation.

Sciens Water is a water-focused private equity firm that was started within Sciens Capital, the New York-based private equity group that has been making buyout investments since 1994 in various industries including manufacturing, service companies, airlines and shipping. Sciens Capital owns Asprey International, the London-based jeweller among other companies.

Alex proceeded to update me on his work and quickly started speaking about water and U.S. water infrastructure as a unique opportunity they were now focused on. He became very enthusiastic sharing about how neglected this rather esoteric sector of the U.S. economy was, and how they had a tremendous opportunity to consolidate various parts of it including undervalued private utilities that needed to be significantly upgraded. He had already invested in a utility that was purchasing smaller utilities which were starved for capital and had not been upgraded. This utility has a great management team and has been making these acquisitions with the goal of creating a leading operator of utilities and potentially selling or taking it public in the future. Alex was not only enthusiastic about making good investments for his limited partners, he was committed and passionate about upgrading America's infrastructure.

I had been away from making private equity investments for over 16 years, and I was surprised at how excited he was about having a significant positive impact on society and the environment beyond financial returns. I don't remember ever having conversations about impact like this in my days in private equity. Alex emphasized how outrageous it was to have these incredibly neglected water systems, and how millions of Americans are suffering as a result. Alex decided to focus exclusively at identifying opportunities to invest in the upgrading and consolidation of different segments in U.S. water infrastructure. I learned that in the segment of water utilities, there are over 52,000 separate water systems. The United Kingdom has 14.[1] A large portion of these are private and are bringing water to the homes of Americans outside of the traditional municipal water utilities.

We saw that together we could bring philanthropy to his private equity strategy to purchase, upgrade and consolidate some of the most neglected and struggling of these private water utilities and in the process deliver clean water to American homes. It is estimated that at least 21 million people have polluted water in their home, but the number may be as high as 150 million with up to half of the water in American homes potentially polluted![2] Nationally well-known tragedies like Flint, IN, and Newark, NJ, and leading water advocates like Erin Brockovich, have allowed people to realize the severity of this issue. Nevertheless, no one I have met outside this specialized industry realize how abandoned our country's water infrastructure is. Government spending has been meagre in water for decades and many of these smaller private systems have found themselves in financial distress, unable to self-finance or access capital markets to upgrade their systems. Thus, they are receiving regular violations for contaminants in their water.

As Alex described the industry, he also mentioned that there were over 5,000 utilities in the U.S. that were in areas with extremely low incomes, with truly abandoned utilities which required very significant investments to get them upgraded making them uneconomical for Sciens. Because of this, Sciens could not purchase them as they didn't meet the minimum investment goals. By the time they purchased and made the larger than average upgrades to these utilities, there was not much (if any) profit left and so the residents were stuck with polluted water at home. Alex was frustrated with this tragedy.

These are utilities with the most polluted water in American homes. Sciens has a very large universe of potential acquisition targets but must ultimately ignore these highly distressed, abandoned and stranded ones. They understand that they could deliver clean water but they can't go out of business doing so as their limited partners expect market private equity returns. They could also consider raising prices post-acquisition and upgrade, but these communities cannot sustain them. These utilities are stranded as the political will to upgrade them with tax revenue is not there and they are not economically viable investments for private investors to purchase and upgrade.

From a social justice lens, these utilities are in areas of struggling economies, high poverty, and high unemployment. They are also large examples of environmental racism and inequality, and therefore, very clear and visible opportunities to generate enormous social justice impact. From our very first discussion, it was obvious to Alex and me that there may be a clear opportunity to meet the needs of all the stakeholders by blending large philanthropy into these potential acquisitions. If philanthropy could pay for enough of the upgrade costs of these utilities, they could be purchased and upgraded while meeting the minimum return of the Sciens portfolio company.

As we started working towards this goal, it became increasingly clear that using a Donor Advised Fund could be a vehicle to deploy larger amounts of philanthropy in a more efficient way than has been seen. This is simply pointing out the obvious. If the nonprofit world has been starved for resources to the extent that taking in $600 billion of philanthropy for rapid scale is not possible, then co-investing philanthropy into for-profit situations that are highly replicable is the answer. Also all the impact is delivered by for-profit management teams that, unlike those at nonprofits, have received all the investments needed for decades. They are eager to receive more funds to do more of what they already do. In addition, many, like Alex and his team, are genuinely enthusiastic to be able to generate very large and visible impact along the way.

Our goal in this sector is to find a philanthropist to make the first investment into one of these distressed utilities. We decided to use a utility in Kentucky as our first investment model and we concluded that a one-time $12 million investment of philanthropy would make it economical to purchase and upgrade. 11,000 residents in that area of Kentucky would see a drastic improvement in their water quality. Then, we can look at replicating this impact with the next of 5,000 possible ones.

From the point of view of creating a vehicle that can deploy large philanthropy effectively, this is it. Given the capital-intensive nature of water infrastructure, we could continue to replicate this investment as Sciens is planning on consolidating hundreds if not thousands of these utilities. If we assumed $10 million would be an average philanthropic investment to make an acquisition and upgrade possible, then 100 of the 5,000 acquisitions would represent $1 billion in philanthropy. This could be attained by Sciens in a handful of years. Their portfolio company is already making and absorbing acquisitions of the other utilities that they can purchase meeting their minimum return. They are closing on acquisitions on a regular basis.

1,000 acquisitions would require $10 billion of philanthropy, and so on. All 5,000 would require about $50 billion which is still less than 10% of The Giving Pledge funds. The key is finding the first philanthropist and proving the approach using a for-profit to generate very high sustainable impact that is immensely replicable, and, where our partners were ready to make many more acquisitions. The next step would be lining up more philanthropic investors who would want to attain great scale. We can also attract government grants which can use this approach to deliver upgraded utilities and clean water. Decentralized water systems would also be used to compliment utility upgrades on a sustainable basis.

Many of the other areas of U.S. water infrastructure that need upgrading are also causing acute harm at a high cost. Sciens has already purchased companies in the water storage and wastewater companies and is consolidating those areas. Considering that 46% of U.S. rivers are polluted,[3] we are very interested in seeing how philanthropy can accelerate the cleaning of rivers and the runoffs to oceans.

We plan to grow a team of investment professionals to make these co-investments. Groups like Sciens will be leading the projects while we review these deals, asking for impact as part of our investments, ensuring it can be delivered, overseeing the impact long term and collecting and reporting on the impact data. We will also be working to engage donors and their families in our work and in advocating for this new approach to others who may be frustrated with their current philanthropic impact or who appreciate the innovation at an enormous scale.

As we close the first investment, we will also be advocating for this co-investing strategy as a very effective way to deliver impact by funding acquisitions with government grants. President Biden's administration is actively moving to upgrade water infrastructure, which is in crisis. Our approach can first unlock significant philanthropic capital, and then, could unlock much larger government funds so they can be deployed in a targeted, measurable, sustainable and effective way. As we move towards funding a large-scale solution of delivering clean drinking water in specific areas, it is clear that scale in the delivery of capital is essential. Private for-profits management teams that are incentivized already to rapidly deploy funds in highly accountable processes are ideally suited to deploy billions of philanthropy and government tax funds.

Actively managed philanthropy can thus step into cases like this and solve national and global challenges that will otherwise continue to be neglected. Just as there is a growing track record of government performance contracts with nonprofit providers, our approach can be the next wave of using philanthropy innovations to solve some of our dire problems. Using for-profits to solve challenges traditionally solved by governments may be the best way to encourage government investments at much higher levels. Investing government funds for impact through our private partners could also be an efficient way to maintain accountability for impact in these one-time investments.

Letting go of the familiar path of traditional infrastructure investing, private equity and philanthropy can create this new path to deliver targeted good at scale.

Notes

1. Four U.K.-Based Water Utilities Downgraded on Tougher Regulations; Two Put on Watch Negative; Four Outlooks Negative, Matan Benjamin, February 25, 2020, S&P Global Ratings, https://www.unitedutilities.com/globalassets/z_corp orate-site/investors-pages/25-february-standard-and-poors-rating-report.pdf.
2. 21 million Americans don't have access to safe drinking water. That can put them at higher risk of getting COVID-19, Holly Secon Havovi, Business Insider, July 12, 2020, https://www.businessinsider.in/science/news/21-million-americans-dont-have-access-to-safe-drinking-water-that-can-put-them-at-higher-risk-of-getting-covid-19-/articleshow/76925961.cms.
3. The National Rivers and Streams Assessment 2008/2009, The United States Environmental Protection Agency, https://www.epa.gov/sites/production/files/2016-03/documents/fact_sheet_draft_variation_march_2016_revision.pdf.

"I cannot tell if what the world considers "happiness" is happiness or not. All I know is that when I consider the way they go about attaining it, I see them carried away headlong...All the while they claim to be just on the point of attaining happiness."
—Thomas Merton

16

Philanthropy in Housing Deals

In the nonprofit world, many organizations claim they are working to end the challenge they are dedicated to solve, no matter how limited their resources or reach are. In the fight against homelessness, the term "solving homelessness" is commonly used by nonprofits. There was always a hope that homelessness could be solved. The fact that there are one million homeless Americans living in the U.S. is hard to process. The fact that every city in the U.S. has dozens or hundreds of families, mostly singles moms, living in their cars tonight with their children is shocking. 20,000 children age out of foster care every year when they turn 18 years old and 40–50% of them will become homeless.[1]

Human trafficking is also an appalling reality in every city in the U.S. Domestic violence and other forms of abuse continue unchecked. Nonprofits are overwhelmed and cannot meet a fraction of the demand in most cases. Their staffs are very dedicated yet overrun by needs, a lack of funding and an inability to scale. These are all complex social crises that require high levels of funding and institutional commitment for any progress to occur.

A large common denominator, and the most capital-intensive piece, to the solution of these issues is affordable housing. Most of the housing targeting these issues today is not long-term, permanent affordable housing. They are mostly the traditional short-term housing shelters, or short-term supportive housing, which means a form of housing with more supportive services including mental health, education and job training. The challenge with this form of housing and the challenge with providing more of it is that it is not self-sufficient and mostly short-term. It is funded by philanthropy and government grants that need to be replenished every year, and those exiting are mostly not tracked, nor do they have stable housing at exit to know how effective the short-term housing is. Permanent affordable housing is long-term and allows for the residents to be tracked year after year to measure success.

Most nonprofits, even very large ones in the U.S., are run on a one-year budget. There is too much management focus on helping clients, and "keeping the lights on," to focus much on adding more housing, which is wildly time consuming, and ultimately creates added pressure to raise more money to cover increases in costs to manage, run and maintain new housing. This is not a sustainable model, especially with limited government resources and nonprofits operating with limited resources.

I was introduced to the concept of financially sustainable affordable housing for the homeless in 2016 at a Palm Beach County sponsored housing summit. The concept was simple: apply for large government tax credit funds to build affordable housing and rent apartments at different rent levels in order to guarantee that all the ongoing costs of the buildings were covered. I saw the leadership of Carrefour, a nonprofit affordable housing developer based in Miami, present the concept. They had successfully built over 18 of these buildings across three counties in South Florida and they were each self-sufficient. The mixed-rents approach even covered the added services that they provided residents in terms of mental health reminders and support.

This was a game-changer. There were $10 million tax credit government grants available regularly across the U.S. to build this kind of affordable housing on a competitive basis. Some of these developers competing for these funds were nonprofits and some were for-profits. In addition, the mixed rents of the buildings allowed market or near market residents to support residents who required more affordable rents. These are also beautiful buildings that look and feel like most of the equivalent market rate developments in each area.

Obtaining the tax-credit funds is a competitive process. Managing the whole process is complex and challenging and it is what these specialized developers focus on to help finance their buildings. It is the future in terms of adding more housing for vulnerable populations and for working Americans as a whole. There is an affordable housing crisis for all income levels but especially for those with lower income and those in vulnerable populations such as the homeless, youth ageing out of foster care, victims of domestic violence, and human trafficking victims. Rents have skyrocketed and outstripped any increases in income. In 2017, almost 38 million households (and 31.5% of total households) experienced very high cost-burdened in that 30% or more of their income went to pay rent, according to Harvard University's Joint Center for Housing Studies.[2]

While working for homeless nonprofits, I led the development of the first housing unit for single homeless women in Palm Beach County. I learned that this 10 bed residential facility was the only place that a single woman could be housed in a county with over 1.5 million residents. There was very limited housing for male individuals and for families. But if you were a single woman, there was nowhere to go aside for a few beds that were available for victims of domestic violence. It was an incredible amount of work as we didn't have a real estate or construction management department. All the work of finding a property and managing the renovation project was simply added to the fundraising process. Otherwise, it would not be done, and at the end of the project, we could only hope to raise the added funds to our annual budget to keep its doors open.

It was a success, a beautiful building adding the first beds to house single homeless women in the county, while also resulting in excellent board and major donor engagement and funding. It later led to additional buildings but I was oblivious to a still better model. A similar amount of work could generate 300 units with 900 beds for the amount of work as the 10 beds of supportive housing we brought online. I also realized that our county had been effectively "missing out" on any tax credit funding for decades as no one knew how or had the capacity to develop these tax credit buildings.

In 2015, I had developed Merton's first "Big Bet" plan to add 500 permanent affordable housing apartments for formerly homeless individuals, by expanding, Community Partners, a local nonprofit which already had 80 apartments. These individuals were the "frequent-users" of the system, meaning those who regularly visited the emergency rooms, the jail or the homeless shelters. The Corporation for Supportive Housing (the leading national homelessness research and consulting nonprofit) had conducted several studies of these individuals nationally. One of these studies was being done in Palm Beach County already. Our goal was to house these individuals while eliminating costs in the system and have some of those cost savings paid back to make the nonprofit sustainable.

Our "if you build it they will come" strategy for this $85 million philanthropic expansion was one-of-a-kind in scale and impact. Unfortunately, as discussed previously, despite having an excellent CEO and management team, it was almost entirely funded with government grants so there were no major donors to rally around this project.

Nevertheless, the local unit of The Salvation Army was interested in creating a similar large-scale plan that could be replicated in other parts of the country. We concluded that after a year of work that the tax credit route was not a fit with The Salvation Army's internal approval process. The head of our local unit, Pierre Smith, liked to say "the Army has two speeds, slow and slower." It was a great opportunity though of seeing a multi-billion dollar operation from the inside. The Army has some of the most hard-working, dedicated and humble individuals I have ever met.

As I looked at the affordable housing market again, in light or our water infrastructure work with Sciens Water and the Columbia Water Center at Columbia University, it became apparent to me that blending very large philanthropy into for-profit affordable housing could also work to fund the needed housing in the U.S. Whether the tax credit funds were secured by a for-profit or a nonprofit developer, the buildings still needed to be fully self-sufficient. I concluded that we would be able to unlock great amounts of impact by adding philanthropy in these housing deals. Developers in turn would be able to bring much more affordable housing online.

The Tamer Center for Social Enterprise at Columbia University provided MBA interns for us in our water infrastructure work in 2019, as well as six MBA interns for the summer of 2020 that were funded by their fellowships. Two of these interns were tasked with tracking down and setting up calls with the top national developers of affordable housing.

We had several conversations with these leading developers to explore if and how they would be interested in receiving philanthropic investments into their projects. The idea of philanthropic investments is something they had not explored in this way that made their traditional affordable housing model have more impact. They had hundreds of family offices making impact investments into their projects on a for-profit basis, but we wanted to see how much more impact we could generate with philanthropy beyond filling in any gap financing to build more traditional tax credit financed buildings. It became clear that there was interest from developers and that philanthropy could make them more likely to be awarded the tax credits in these competitive processes. The philanthropy could also provide more services for their clients as well as act as "gap financing" to help close deals. I felt this kind of financing is hard to get but already available and that we wanted to generate impact beyond their traditional formats.

We had extensive conversations with two groups, one in Florida, and one in Indiana, who are major affordable housing players. They both provided us with actual tax credit projects they were developing which had already won the government process. We looked at the project details and plans and thought about how to invest the philanthropy. Many of the discussions were about setting up a rent subsidy fund that could reduce rents for clients every year. This was closer to the traditional nonprofit model and would require fundraising on an ongoing basis.

It became clear that we could replace about $10 million in debt with a loan from our DAF with no interest funded by a philanthropist we would attract. Nearly $500,000 in annual interest expense could be then used to reduce rents permanently. This would be a one-time investment that permanently changes the project's capital structure. It was surprising that even though these projects were very time intensive and complex, only 15% of their final units are considered to be "deeply affordable" and available to vulnerable populations at about $450 a month. The rest were $1,000 or $1,250 and above. This was, of course, necessary to generate the cash flows to cover all the expenses, including the interest expense. With our approach, the number of apartments that were at the $450 a month rate would permanently increase to 45%, generating an increase of 300% in impact.

Of course, the developers were interested in generating more impact to help the local communities where they were going to continue to be active in. Local mayors would also be delighted with this as the area of most affordable housing need is in this area for more vulnerable populations. An example would be a single mother with two kids who suffers from a debilitating case of PTSD after her service in Iraq. Without this deeply discounted permanent affordable housing, they would be living in their car, in a friend's couch or in homeless shelters.

This 300% impact is generated while the developer makes the same return, and nothing else changes in the buildings. If a philanthropist funded this investment and wanted to focus more on a particular vulnerable population that required more services, we would include this in the cash flows and would hire or outsource the management of this to specialized staff. The Carrefour success rates are astonishing. They naturally track their residents and their formerly homeless residents which is what they focus on have year-over-year retention rates of 96%. This is the solution for homelessness that needs to be scaled up.

According to the Corporation for Supportive Housing, affordable housing providers often reach retention rates above 80%. So the question is "how do we do more of this?" A simple approach is to make similar philanthropic co-investments into existing affordable housing projects. Every year, 1,000 of these are funded with tax credit funds. We believe we can invest $3 billion a year in philanthropy into their projects. They are happening anyways, so why not increase their impact by 300%? We would also look to transform their environmental impact in terms of reducing their greenhouse gas emissions with decarbonization strategies. This would be environmental impact at scale too.

The real interesting change comes when we use more of The Giving Pledge funds to go beyond this 300% increase in impact in the affordable housing already being developed. We can target specific solutions that are needed and fund the affordable housing in clusters of buildings in specific areas. For example, if there are 200 women with children living in their cars in Houston every night, we can provide the philanthropy for developers to deliver two buildings to entirely house this population in any given night. We can then celebrate that solution and replicate it nationally. These would be mainly built in addition to the 1,000 buildings being built annually with tax-credit funds, which are limited and exhausted every year. Philanthropy would replace the tax credit funding in each building, and the developers are happy to build more to get this done.

We believe that philanthropists will find this approach very attractive to leverage for-profit developers who can rapidly increase their teams to take on more buildings. The implications for solving some of the most challenging social issues in the U.S. are game-changing. These new buildings can also be deployed into place-based initiatives in cities coordinating new housing with early learning to be housed in the buildings in addition to job training programs, health care providers and others to drive solutions. Place-based initiatives are key to turning around neighborhoods and distressed urban areas.

Affordable housing is the cornerstone for critical solutions for many of our specific challenges and for poverty in general. There are so many initiatives to reduce poverty and coordinate services but there is a critical lack of large-scale funding and scalability. We are looking to provide the funding by giving philanthropists an opportunity to roll-out thousands of buildings with incredible impact. By partnering with for-profit developers (and some large nonprofit ones), we can deploy large amounts of The Giving Pledge funds in similar strategies.

Notes

1. Foster Care and Homelessness, Shalita O'Neale, Foster Focus, Volume 5 Issue 3, https://www.fosterfocusmag.com/articles/foster-care-and-homelessness#:~:text=More%20recent%20statistics%20include%20the%20following%3A&text=Approximately%20400%2C000%20youth%20are%20currently,any%20family%20connection%20at%20all.&text=Within%2018%20months%20of%20emancipation,of%20foster%20youth%20become%20homeless.

2. Nearly a Third of American Households Were Cost-Burdened Last Year, Sean Veal, Jonathan Spader, December 7, 2018, Harvard University Joint Center for Housing Studies, https://www.jchs.harvard.edu/blog/more-than-a-third-of-american-households-were-cost-burdened-last-year.

"Yet the fact remains that we are invited to forget ourselves on purpose, cast our awful solemnity to the winds and join in the general dance."
— Thomas Merton

Epilogue

Like the tide pushing a river to flood its banks, the rising tide of good will change the field of large philanthropy. The world of corporate philanthropy and corporate social impact will provide an increased flow of funds into solutions, and large philanthropy will be deployed as highly replicable program related investments into later stage companies. This tide will be encouraged to rise further as ESG ratings are made more sophisticated, refined and more widely utilized by investors. Solution-based investing, will also drive ESG depth and weight, further encouraging corporate philanthropy as well as encouraging Giving Pledge philanthropy towards solutions. Additionally, government funds will also be deployed in these large-scale targeted solutions and make up for the fact that some of our challenges resulted in many years of limited government spending in these areas of need. Affordable housing, water infrastructure, and clean energy are all examples where large philanthropy can be the catalyst to use private industry, and especially later stage companies, as the delivery mechanism for impact and for solving entire challenges.

The key question is how do we encourage the signers of The Giving Pledge and the 2,600 other billionaires to give more? This may happen more quickly at the next level wealth, the 150,000 individuals in the world with $100 million or more. A better question is how do we listen to their needs, create deals that are attractive for them to fund and can be exceptionally fulfilling? As Bill and Melinda Gates, MacKenzie Scott, Chuck Harris, Olivia Leland, Richard Branson and other pioneers in this space work to solve this question, we all have to be creating win-win opportunities for them and everyone else.

© The Editor(s) (if applicable) and The Author(s), under exclusive
license to Springer Nature Switzerland AG 2021
S. Davis, *Solving the Giving Pledge Bottleneck*,
https://doi.org/10.1007/978-3-030-78865-0

The gifting of fortunes, if realized, creates the opportunity to fund teams that can deliver solutions through later stage companies. We move large philanthropy from discussions about funding organizations, measuring outputs, outcomes and impact, to measuring and funding actual solutions for all of our main social and environmental challenges. All the stakeholders benefit directly.

The rising tide of good will continue to come in and will accelerate. New challenges will emerge including unintended consequences of new approaches to doing good. Nevertheless, this is exciting, and will accelerate all of social impact in ways we have yet to see and we just need to continue to push on, each of us in our own way, to forge the path forward, even as we don't know exactly where it is going.

As Thomas Merton emphasized to the novices at the Abbey of Gethsemani: "You do not need to know precisely what is happening, or exactly where it is all going. What you need is to recognize the possibilities and challenges offered by the present moment, and to embrace them with courage, faith, and hope."

Index

© The Editor(s) (if applicable) and The Author(s), under exclusive license to Springer Nature Switzerland AG 2021
S. Davis, *Solving the Giving Pledge Bottleneck*,
https://doi.org/10.1007/978-3-030-78865-0